Hans-Martin Zademach

Spatial Dynamics in the Markets of M&A

Essays on the Geographical Determination and Implications of Corporate Takeovers and Mergers in Germany and Europe

Herbert Utz Verlag · VVF · München

Wirtschaft und Raum

Eine Reihe der Münchener Universitätsschriften

herausgegeben von

Prof. Dr. Hans-Dieter Haas
Universität München

Band 12

Zugl.: Diss., München, Univ., 2005

Bibliografische Information Der Deutschen Bibliothek:
Die Deutsche Bibliothek verzeichnet diese Publikation
in der Deutschen Nationalbibliografie;
detaillierte bibliografische Daten sind im Internet über
http://dnb.ddb.de abrufbar.

Dieses Werk ist urheberrechtlich geschützt.
Die dadurch begründeten Rechte, insbesondere die
der Übersetzung, des Nachdrucks, der Entnahme von
Abbildungen, der Wiedergabe auf photomechanischem oder ähnlichem Wege und der Speicherung in
Datenverarbeitungsanlagen bleiben – auch bei nur
auszugsweiser Verwendung – vorbehalten.

Copyright © Herbert Utz Verlag GmbH · 2005

ISBN 3-8316-0478-9

Printed in Germany

Herbert Utz Verlag GmbH, München
089-277791-00 · www.utzverlag.de

GELEITWORT

Fusionen und Unternehmenskäufe (Mergers & Acquisitions, abgekürzt M&A) gelten in der Wissenschaft – vor allem aus der Sicht der raumwissenschaftlichen Forschung – als ein immer noch sehr stark vernachlässigter Untersuchungsgegenstand. Dabei kommen in der jüngeren Vergangenheit nationalen und grenzüberschreitenden Unternehmenszusammenschlüssen sowie -übernahmen eine herausragende Bedeutung zu. Das betrifft nicht nur die Fallzahlen, sondern auch die Transaktionsvolumina. Vor allem in den 1990er Jahren und um die Wende ins neue Jahrtausend gab es weltweit einen förmlichen M&A-Boom. Innerhalb der beteiligten Unternehmen lösen Fusionen und Akquisitionen umfangreiche Reorganisationsprozesse aus. Diese wiederum haben beachtliche gesamtwirtschaftliche Auswirkungen. Dabei werden ebenso wirtschaftsräumliche Strukturen und raumspezifische Prozesse deutlich verändert. Regionale Struktureffekte können sich allein schon aus den Veränderungen lokaler Arbeitsmärkte ergeben oder durch den Transfer wissensintensiver Unternehmenseinheiten. Vor allem sog. Mega-Fusionen, wie z.b. die Übernahme von Mannesmann durch Vodafone, lösen in der Regel größere raumstrukturelle Folgewirkungen aus.

Wegen des schwierigen Zugangs zu sensiblen Geschäftsdaten gibt es bis in die allerjüngste Zeit nur ganz wenige wissenschaftliche Untersuchungen auf breiter empirischer Basis; dies gilt insbesondere für regionalwirtschaftliche bzw. wirtschaftsgeographische Analysen. Umso dringlicher besteht gerade hier ein enormer Forschungsbedarf. Mit der vorliegenden Arbeit gelingt es Hans-Martin Zademach, diese Forschungslücke mit detaillierten wissenschaftlichen Analysen ein Stück weit zu schließen. Er legt im Rahmen eines kumulativen Promotionsverfahrens drei von einander unabhängige, in sich geschlossene Papers vor, die alle der o.g. M&A-Thematik zuzuordnen sind. Diese Essays wenden sich dem Themenkreis aus jeweils unterschiedlicher Perspektive zu. Ziel ist es vor allem, M&A-Transaktionen auf verschiedenen Maßstabsebenen hinsichtlich ihrer Distanzabhängigkeit und raumstruktureller Wirkungen zu erforschen und zu bewerten. So werden generell Erkenntnisse darüber gewonnen, welches Gewicht raumspezifische Faktoren bei Fusions- und Akquisitionsvorgängen besitzen und welche Rolle diese bei unternehmensstrategischen Entscheidungen spielen. Mit Hilfe sekundärstatistischer und ergänzender primärstatistischer Untersuchungen werden grundlegende standort- und raumrelevante Fragen, die im Rahmen der wichtig gewordenen M&A-Forschung heute vermehrt auftreten, schlüssig beantwortet: Sind M&A-Prozesse standortunabhängig und quasi nicht-räumlich? Welche Standortfaktoren bestimmen Übernahmeentscheidungen und worin liegt genau der Einfluss von räumlicher Nähe, welche Bedeutung haben Agglomerationseffekte oder lokalisierte Ressourcen? Seine Antworten bringen die Wissenschaft in diesem Bereich deutlich weiter.

Die drei im Band enthaltenen Beiträge sind von ihrer wissenschaftstheoretischen Fundierung originell und originär, gleichzeitig aber auch sehr sorgfältig angelegt. Sie orientieren sich an der aktuellen Forschungsfront und greifen über die engen Fachgrenzen hinweg. Aus fachmethodologischer Sicht stellt sich in den Beiträgen jeweils auch die Frage, wie sich diese Thematik in den raumwirtschaftlichen bzw. relationalen Forschungsansatz der Wirtschaftsgeographie einbringen lässt und wie möglicherweise eine Integration eben dieser wirtschaftswissenschaftlichen und sozialwissenschaftlichen Perspektive aussehen könnte. Zademach hat mit seinen Forschungen die mikrotheoretische Fundierung des Faches erweitert und mit seiner Anlehnung an organisationstheoretische Unternehmenskonzeptionen zugleich auch der betriebswirtschaftlichen Perspektive in der Wirtschaftsgeographie verstärkt Bedeutung beigemessen. Indem unterschiedliche Forschungsansätze zusammengeführt und mit bestehenden Zugängen zur Theorie der Unternehmung verbunden werden, leistet die vorliegende Arbeit einen anspruchsvollen und wichtigen Beitrag zur aktuellen Forschung im Bereich der Wirtschaftsgeographie im Speziellen und den Wirtschaftswissenschaften im Allgemeinen.

Der Herausgeber   München, im November 2005

PREFACE

The contribution in hand results from my time as research and teaching assistant at the Institute of Economic Geography in the Munich School of Management, Ludwig-Maximilians-University. First of all, I express my gratitude to my appreciated professor and supervisor Hans-Dieter Haas for his constant advice and inspiration. Probably not despite, but by virtue of our sometimes rather controversial content-specific views leading to a series of fruitful debates, he invariably personified a consistently critical instance and therefore an irreplaceable guide for my personal development as young academic. Professor Arnold Picot is thanked for taking over the co-report as well as his support and incitements throughout the whole project. I could benefit from the spirited and gratefully acknowledged attitude towards the novel of a cumulative doctoral thesis of both of them.

Likewise, I am deeply indebted to Andrés Rodríguez-Pose as an additional prime intellectual mentor. Since completing my studies in his MSc-programme in 2001, he became more than a colleague and scholarly companion for me, but simply a friend. Here in Munich, I am grateful to all colleagues at the Institute of Economic Geography, most notably Johannes, Martin, Karl and Daniel. All of them represented constructive commentators and became much valued mates which acted in exactly that way.

Special thanks are also due to German higher education policies not to be omitted here. Lacking all the turbulences while compiling this work, its completion would definitively have taken another good deal of time. Tailwind, on the other hand, came from the anonymous referees providing a positive appraisal of the first, already submitted paper as well as Förderverein Kurt Fordan für herausragende Begabungen and the German Research Foundation DFG. In excess of the monetary sponsorship, I am grateful to the latter institution for the important mental back-up signalled through the agreement on the proposal for a greater research project, parts of which are reflected in this collection.

Without the help of Steffen Mezger and Peter Germonpre ("I owe you something, bro's") who gave access to sensitive M&A data the research could not have been conducted. The same is true with regard to the experts interviewed – I am thankful to all of them for the time and efforts they devoted to the project. My current collegiate assistants Julius, Manuel and Philipp as well as 'Hadschi' and Matthias as former back staff are acknowledged for their altruistic endeavours, including their outstanding engagement for the discipline and the future of the Institute and its diploma-programme – aiming always to remember how much can be learned from them, in fact, I am indebted to all our economic geography students, especially 'my' graduates, of whom I wish to mention Petzi, Tom, Pat and Matthias by name. Sincere thanks also to Adala, Vassilis and Beniad for being exciting conversation partners during my several stays in London as well as the fellow students of the MBR-programme, most notably Hannes and Caro as indispensable combatants in our 'campaigns' in the last month. Franz Eder is thanked for his great quality work on the maps as well as for the kind help he and his colleague Heinz Sladkowski gave on all research projects conducted during my time at the Institute.

I finally want to ask my friends Champi, Mathias and the two Robert Hubers along all the ones not explicitly mentioned here to accept my apologies for certainly having disregarded them too heavily when finishing this piece of work and express my deepest gratitude to my family for all their backing, affirmations and sunshine.

Munich, October 2004   Hans-Martin Zademach

CONTENTS

Geleitwort des Herausgebers V
Preface VII
Contents IX
List of Figures XII
List of Tables XIII
Abbreviations XIV

1 INTRODUCTION 1

  **1.1 Sketching the conceptual formulation –
      M&As as a 'non-spatial' phenomenon out of place?** 1

  1.2 Organisation and structure of compilation 3

**2 M&A, ECONOMIC DEVELOPMENT AND URBAN REGIONS:
  THE GERMAN EXPERIENCE** 7

  2.1 Analytical framework 9

  2.2 Territorial distribution and flows of M&As in Germany ... 14
      2.2.1 Spatial distribution of M&As in Germany 16
      2.2.2 Spaces of flows in the German market of M&A 20

  2.3 The factors shaping the geography of M&As in Germany ... 23
      2.3.1 Individual regressions: Agglomeration vs. proximity 24
      2.3.2 Multiple regression analysis 31

  2.4 Conclusions 38

**3 GEOGRAPHICAL DYNAMICS IN THE OLD AND NEW ECONOMY -
  THE MARKETS OF M&A IN GERMANY** 41

  3.1 Corporate takeovers in spatial perspective 42
      3.1.1 Key factors underlying the most recent wave of M&As ... 43

  3.1.2 Spatial and developmental implications of M&As:
    On corporate control and metropolitan systems 44
  3.1.3 Takeovers and mergers on the academic research agenda 46
  3.1.4 Differing location specifics in differing economies 47
  3.1.5 Corporate takeovers and economic geography –
    a relational perception.. 48
3.2 The reshaping of economic activity in Germany by means of M&As 49
  3.2.1 Data and methodology 50
  3.2.2 An emerging archipelago economy? 52
  3.2.3 The territorial dynamics of M&As in Germany 54
3.3 Industry specifics in German takeover activity... 58
  3.3.1 Classifying the markets of M&As 58
  3.3.2 New economy 63
  3.3.3 Old economy 66
3.4 Conclusions 67

**4 THE CHANGING ECONOMIC GEOGRAPHY OF EUROPE:
EVIDENCE FORM M&A ACTIVITIES 69**
4.1 On firms, M&As and economic integration.. 72
  4.1.1 Conceptualising the firm in economic geographical terms 75
  4.1.2 Contextual influences as determinants of firms and M&As..... 78
  4.1.3 Cross-border investments in the light of regional integration ... 80
4.2 Methodological foundations and specification of analysis 81
  4.2.1 Data description and preparation 82
  4.2.2 Formalisation of the spatial determination of M&As............... 84
**4.3 The changing Economic Geography of Europe – Insights from the
descriptive examinations... 87**

    4.3.1 Preliminary observations 87
    4.3.2 Cross-border M&A activities 91
4.4 The link between M&As and the new face of Europe: Regression results **94**
4.5 Conclusions **100**

5 FINAL CONSOLIDATION AND CONCLUDING REMARKS **102**
5.1 A place for space in M&As? **102**
5.2 Contributions to the existing literature **103**

REFERENCES **105**

APPENDIX **117**

LIST OF FIGURES

Fig. 2.1:   Merging/acquiring firms per Regierungsbezirk 17
Fig. 2.2:   Spatial distribution of M&A targets acquired from most important German metropoli 21
Fig. 3.1:   Acquiring firms and M&A targets in Germany 1990-94 54
Fig. 3.2:   Acquiring firms and M&A targets in Germany 1995-99 56
Fig. 3.3:   The changing relevance of agglomeration economies and geographical distance in the German M&A economy 57
Fig. 3.4:   M&A specificities across German industry sectors: Economies of proximity vs. metropolitan interconnectivity 59
Fig. 3.5:   M&A specificities across German industry sectors: Results of the yearly regressions 60
Fig. 4.1:   Trends in M&A activities involving European firms (1998-2003) 69
Fig. 4.2:   Conceptual framework to analyse the implications and determination of firms and M&As 75
Fig. 4.3:   The European market of corporate takeovers at global scales (by number of events) 86
Fig. 4.4:   The European market of corporate takeovers at global scales (by volume of transactions) 88
Fig. 4.5:   Territorial distribution of acquiring firms and M&A targets in Europe, 1998-2003 (by number of events) 90
Fig. 4.6:   Territorial distribution of acquiring firms and M&A targets in Europe, 1998-2003 (by volume of transactions) 92
Fig. 4.7:   Cross-border interactions in the markets of M&As in Europe 94

LIST OF TABLES

Tab. 2.1:	M&As taking place from the six most important German metropoli regressed on the independent variables	26
Tab. 2.2:	Explaining takeover activities in the German key nodes of M&A	32
Tab. 3.1:	The German markets of M&As: Classification of industries	63
Tab. 4.1:	Aggregate volumes and mean deal values of domestic, intra-European and and intercontinental M&As involving firms based in Europe	71
Tab. 4.2:	Description of Mergermarket database as prepared for the analysis	83
Tab. 4.3:	M&A activities in Europe: Estimates of robust Poisson regressions on number of events	96
Tab. 4.4:	M&A activities in Europe: Results of OLS regressions on volumes in logarithmic form	97

LIST OF ABBREVIATIONS

EFTA	European Free Trade Association
EU	European Union
EMU	European Monetary Union
FDI	Foreign Direct Investment
ICT	Information and Communication Technologies
GDP	Gross Domestic Product
M&A	Mergers and Acquisitions
MNC	Multinational Corporations
OECD	Organisation for Economic Co-operation and Development
OLS	Ordinary Least Square
R&D	Research and Development
SEM	Single European Market
UN	United Nations
UNCTAD	United Nations Conference on Trade and Development
WTO	World Trade Organisation

1 INTRODUCTION

High levels of mergers and acquisitions (M&As) have been a characteristic of the global economy in the 1990s and at the turn of the millennium. This wave of M&As did not only lead to important modifications in the structure of businesses, but also triggered thorough restructuring processes in the location of corporate control and economic decision-making. The spatial implications of corporate takeovers and mergers as well as their location-specific or contextual determination, however, represent profoundly neglected topics in economic geographical research. On an empirical basis, the contribution in hand intends to explore these issues for Germany and Europe.

1.1 Sketching the conceptual formulation – M&As as a 'non-spatial' phenomenon out of place?

Corporations are increasingly engaged in takeover and merger activities in order to enter new markets. The accumulation of M&A transactions since the mid 1980s has been accompanied by profiled restructuring processes of the corporate landscape, alongside partly substantial reactions of international financial markets (cf. Gugler et al. 2003; Böhmer and Löffler 1999; Loughran and Vij 1997; Gerke et al. 1995; Healy 1992, amongst others). Territorial displacement and relocation of corporate control and decision-making functions on the microeconomic level represent further important consequences of the latest wave of M&As. By means of their ramifications on the spatial organisation of production, the coalescence of two firms or the absorption of one corporation by another one sustainably shape a nation's texture of corporate locations.

The transfer of knowledge-intensive business units or changes of local labour markets represent examples for the mechanisms how the continous high number of transactions in recent years and their often substantial volumes impact on regional production systems. These effects are particularly significant in the event of so-called megamergers such as between Daimler-Benz and Chrysler, for instance, or acquisitions in the dimension of Time Warner (taken over by AOL) or Vodafone-Mannesmann. Within the scope of the acquisition of Aventis – this corporate group arose only in 1999 from a merger of Hoechst and Rhône-Poulenc – by its French competitor Sanofi-

Synthélabo (accredited by the European Commission Directorate-General for Competition in April 2004), it is likewise worried about 9.000 jobs in the Rhine-Main-Area and the drain of its biotechnological know-how to France. On a regular basis, firms referred to as global players act in this manner as multiple buyers; the German electronic group Siemens, for example, undertook worldwide fourteen major acquisitions between 2000 and 2003 alone.

While the literature on the evaluation of companies, on the proceedings or the termination of an M&A transaction, on critical factors of success, pre- and post-merger integration management, the managing of trans- or cross-cultural mergers and so forth multiplied in a hardly manageable manner over the last decade (for an overview, see e.g. Gaughan 2002, Weston et al. 2001 or Jansen 2000), comprehensive and comparative studies focussing on M&As from the specific point of view of spatial sciences are markedly rare. Markusen (2001: 2) points to this disregard in particular explicitness, when asking

> "why recent developments of enormous economic geographical impact such as ... corporate mergers receive such short shrift."

A possible cause for this neglect might be the presumption that spatial systems are not associated with M&As. The first resulting implication, namely that the effects of connected organisational restructuring processes on the intra-firm level do not affect a firm's location region, is yet not maintainable and sufficiently disproved by empirical studies (see Ashcroft and Love 1993 as one example). On the other hand, a negation of an association between M&As and space would imply that the geographical perspective provides no additional explanatory power to the question why companies do acquire a certain target. In the light of recent studies on M&As, which focused most notably on particular ‚big' and – especially in terms of media coverage – 'sensational' mergers and related to cost and revenue oriented motives, at first, this appears to be plausible.

The significant share of M&A transactions, where marketing and distribution goals represent the key motives or the decisive incentives for a merger or an acquisition (e.g. Jansen 2001: 27), however, contradicts this line of argumentation. Suchlike strategic decisions on the subject of market positioning, as to aim for the raise of market shares abroad via a cross-border merger for instance, are characterised by significant spatial constituents (like the evaluation and selection of certain target markets in terms of a corporate regional strategy or the aim to access a certain 'milieu') to which sufficient attention has hitherto not been paid. Against this background, it is essential to apprehend M&A transactions in their entirety and complexity, thus examining the phenomenon e.g. in terms of tall accounts. Therein lies yet another research-pragmatic reason for the neglect of M&As as topic of investigation. As access to data – in this field often utterly sensitive – is very limited, capacious quantitative examinations on corporate takeovers have rarely been possible (Chapman and Edmond 2000; Sachwald 1994).

The few cases of M&A-related investigations in spatial sciences discuss either individual case studies or have an explicit industry focus. In fact, these studies brought forward valuable insights on the reasons why companies engage in a merger, probable internal post-merger effects, or consequential processes of industry restructuring. Furthermore, they gave first indications for M&As indeed affecting space- and place-specific structures and economic systems, like a nation's metropolitan hierarchy or regional disparities (cf. Green 1990), and that corporate takeovers thus impact on more than intra-firm management functions, organisational structures and hierarchies, reporting measures, controlling systems and the like.

The inverse direction of the causal relationship between M&As and 'spaces and places' (Yeung 2001a), i.e. the relevance of space-related attributes as influencing variables in M&A processes, represents an almost completely ignored research topic. The present contribution addresses this issue along with the spatial implications of M&As. Consequently it aims to explore the extent to which location factors determine M&A processes or, in other words, the question of what exactly the leverage effects of geographical proximity, agglomeration economies or localised resources and competencies are when it comes to M&A decision-making. Hence, the twofold aim of the study can be summarised as follows:

- First, to display the implications of M&As, most notably in terms of the shifts and displacement of corporate control they provoke; and
- second, to identify the factors that may explain the detected levels and patterns and the extent to which location factors determine takeover activities and thus firms engaging in M&As.

1.2 Organisation and structure of compilation

The compilation in hand follows the Munich School of Management's regulations of a cumulative doctoral thesis; accordingly, it contains three main chapters. In that way, the chapters represent self-contained and independent essays, each of which is premeditated as autonomous, stand-alone academic piece of work.[1] Their common ground is constituted by the interest and intention to discuss the role of context dependant determinants in corporate mergers or takeovers and the impacts and implications of M&As on spatial structures.[2]

To begin with, the next chapter[3] addresses the interconnections between M&As, economic development and urban regions in Germany. Using three standardized indices representing the relative quantity of takeovers in each German *Regierungsbezirk*, the section initially demonstrates that the recent wave of M&As has resulted in a major concentration of firms and economic activity in the main metropoli of the economy. The chapter then turns to the dynamics of M&A and investigates the flows of transactions in a series of maps. By means of regression analysis, indicators for the general level of agglomeration (i.e. regional GDP and population) and the concentration of political power in the region are identified as main drivers of the geographical concentration of firms. The results also indicate that investment in R&D, the general level of education, or unemployment, when considered in combination with agglomeration indicators, play a negligible role in determining M&A flows. With respect to the geographical distance between a merging or acquiring firm and its target, the results are twofold. While, when estimated on its own, distance has a very weak or – depending on cases – insignificant association with the territorial distribution of M&A activity, proximity appears to play a distinctive role in the geography of M&As in Germany when estimated in conjunction with agglomeration.

The subsequent third chapter explores the thorough reshuffling in the location of economic decision-making through M&As in Germany over the last decade with particular attention being paid to industry-specific transformations. The chapter argues that corporate takeovers have to be conceived as relational processes that show distinctly varying patterns and peculiarities according to their industry characteristics,

---

[1] All three chapters were also submitted to peer-reviewed/refereed journals. In part, the manuscripts have already been accepted for publication.

[2] Though constituency was a central task when completing the compilation, this form of organizing a doctoral thesis may unevitably lead to a certain amount of overlap. The reader is respectfully asked to indulge suchlike intersections, which most notably occur in the context of methodological considerations.

[3] As primal piece of research, this chapter is based on a working paper that meanwhile has been published in *Urban Studies*. Please note, however, that a noticeably different version is given here.

but also depend on their local and institutional contexts. In order to identify the logic behind changes in the location of corporate control and decision-making, the presence of economies of proximity and agglomeration, the degree of metropolitan interconnectivity (or 'archipelago economies'), the concentration of economic activity in large urban metropolitan areas, and the role played by geographical distance in M&As are analysed across ten different industrial sectors. The results signify that a simple 'old' vs. 'new economy' dichotomy is not sufficient to explain the identified changes in the location of economic decision-making and activity across sectors and that the developed classification framework offers more differentiated insights on the dynamics in the German markets of M&As in the 1990s.

Based on the same dataset, the M&A Review database, both the second and the third chapter are limited to the case of Germany. The succeeding fourth section puts its emphasis on the European scale and addresses cross-border transaction in a more explicit manner. It rests upon the encompassing record of M&A activities in Europe by the financial service provider Mergermarket which covers every M&A transaction involving a European firm with an enterprise value of over Euro 5 million from 1998 onwards, as well as on interview-based research at the firm level conducted in London, Copenhagen and selected German sites.

Against the background of economic integration, the fourth chapter examines corporate takeover and merger activities involving firms located in the EU25 and the four EFTA countries between 1998 and 2003, an important period of changes before and after the creation of the European Monetary Union (EMU) and immediately before the Eastern enlargement. First, it identifies the strongest and weakest European economies within the international 'trade' of corporate control in Europe. Thanks to the financial details provided by the Mergermarket data it became possible to consider both the simple counts of events and the respective deal values in this step of the investigation, a novelty in economic geographical research on M&As on the aggregate level. Through the combination of insights from the qualitative research with regression analysis and by means of controlling for the size and economic significance of each transaction, following, the chapter demonstrates the extent to which the spatial perspective sheds light onto the factors that may explain the detected levels and patterns of corporate takeovers across Europe. The results denote that access to new and core markets, effects of geographical proximity as well as access to 'localised capabilities' (approximated via patents per capita as output of a skilled and innovative labour and favourable institutional endowments) represent key drivers in the European M&A economy; institutional affiliations, like the deepened process of European integration, assessments of country risk or linguistic barriers, but also structural factors like e.g. unemployment rates, indeed appear – at least at the intra-European scale – less influential and thus long-term anticipated and already internalised by the market. Albeit the analyses remain in most parts on the aggregated macro-level, conceptualising the firm in micro-theoretical terms as bundle of competencies seeking for the internalisation of localised capabilities can be shown as a promising approach in research on firms and M&As which is relevant not only from the economic geographical viewpoint.

A brief final section provides a final consolidation of the three pieces of work and concludes by underlining the main observations resulting from the hitherto conducted investigations and indicating the study's key contributions to the existing literature.

2 M&A, ECONOMIC DEVELOPMENT AND URBAN REGIONS: THE GERMAN EXPERIENCE[4]

From the beginning of the 1980s onwards there has been a rapid growth and diversification of the literature examining the importance of and the interrelationship between cities in a globalising world (e.g. Braudel 1984; Sassen 1984; Castells 1989). Friedman (1986, 1995) established a global urban hierarchy in which London, New York and Tokyo occupy the top echelon as 'global financial articulations', while other cities, such as Amsterdam or Frankfurt are considered as 'multinational articulations'. Sassen (1991, 2000) regards the dynamism of 'global cities' such as London or 'sub-global cities' (e.g. Frankfurt), as a direct consequence of the spatial dispersion and internalisation of production, leading to the increasing centralisation of the management and regulation of major multinational companies, of financial and business services and government. Global, sub-global and lower rank cities become interrelated in an emerging 'world city network' (Taylor 2001), where the functional links between cities are strengthened beyond physical contiguity (Castells 1996).

Taken to its limits, this interpretation leads to the emergence of what Veltz (1996, 2000) has called an 'archipelago economy', an economy in which the connections between cities with similar roles in a world economy are greatly enhanced, regardless of distance, as they become increasingly detached from their regional and national contexts. This process is driven both by technological and informational change and by, among others, the increasing importance of national and supranational mergers and acquisitions (M&As), which rocketed during the 1990s. This decade saw a wave of acquisition- and merger-driven consolidation throughout the world, accounting for approximately 70% of the total value of inward investment in developed countries, making M&As a more important component than greenfield investments in foreign direct investment (UN 1995).

In contrast to the literature underscoring the links between large urban agglomerations, irrespective of distance, other scholarly research analysing the location of eco-

---

[4]   This chapter is based on common research with Andrés Rodríguez-Pose, Department of Geography and Environment, London School of Economics. His insightful comments are greatfully acknowledged. Gilles Duranton, Johannes Glückler, Murray Low, Dariusz Wójcik and the participants at the *Arbeitskreis Industriegeographie*, Eschwege in November 2002 in Eschwege gave further helpful comments to earlier drafts of this chapter.

nomic activity has tended to draw attention to the role of proximity as a determinant in the development of economic activity. Distance, for example, represents a key factor in geographical economics, where backward and forward linkages and the importance of transportation costs are two important elements behind the strengthening of economic agglomeration (Krugman 1991, 1995; Fujita et al. 1999). Recent literature on innovation has pinpointed the existence of significant distance decay effects affecting, among others, the diffusion of technological spillovers (e.g. Jaffe et al. 1993; Grossman and Helpman 1994; Audretsch and Feldman 1996; Rigby 2000). Also, the identification of the economic importance of untraded interdependencies (Storper 1997) further reinforces the role of physical proximity as a determinant in the location of economic activity.

This chapter looks at these issues in Germany, by focusing on the spatial significance and impact of M&As during the 1990s. Despite the fact that "M&A events are intimately connected to a massive organisational and geographical restructuring" (Dicken and Öberg 1996: 115), the influence of M&As on economic welfare and their spatial implications remain profoundly neglected topics in spatial sciences (see e.g. Dunning 1997 or Markusen 2001). Although there have been some analyses of the spatial impacts of recent waves of M&As (e.g. Green 1990; Ashcroft and Love 1993; Lo 1999, 2000; Aliberti and Green 2000; Chapman and Edmond 2000; Nuhn 2001), these studies have been few and generally tended to focus on specific industries or on large firms for which appropriate data can be compiled (SBA 1998). A major reason for the lack of research into the M&As phenomenon is linked to the limited availability of comprehensive data covering M&As across regions or cities (e.g. Sachwald 1994). The purpose of the study is to partially fill this gap by examining to what extent M&A activity may be considered a major force shaping recent changes in the economic geography of Germany. By analysing the close to 30,000 M&A transactions that took place in Germany between 1990 and 1999 – contained in the M&A Review database – it is tried to explain the recent evolution of the geography of firms in Germany and to identify the factors behind the concentration of economic activity in large urban areas.

The aim of the chapter is thus twofold. First, it examines to what extent urban areas, in general, and large cities in particular, are increasingly becoming the main foci of economic activity as a consequence of the concentration of M&As in cities during the 1990s. Secondly, an assessment is made of the factors associated with the increasing concentration of company headquarters in metropolitan areas. The chapter contains four additional sections. The next section deals with the theoretical foundations of the interlink between firms, M&As and cities. The third section reports the results of the empirical analysis of the data on M&As in Germany, by first identifying the urban agglomerations that have benefited the most from the wave of M&As in the 1990s and then turning to the flows of M&A transactions in each of the top German metropoli. The factors behind the geographical concentration of M&As in Germany are presented in section 2.4. The final section of the chapter provides some concluding remarks.

2.1 Analytical framework

A large body of scientific literature has been built in recent years around the idea that the globalisation of the world economy is associated with the genesis of a new territorial pattern, which basically benefits large urban regions. In Castells (1996) 'space of flows' approach, for instance, world cities are considered as control or command centres within the global network of financial and business firms. Despite the fact that advances in technology and deregulation trends have rendered capital and information highly mobile, empirical studies have stressed how both factors have become increasingly concentrated in large metropolitan areas. It is argued that the expansion of trade and the development of networks is fostering an ever greater urbanisation of capital and decision-making structures and leading to the concentration of wealth and production (Sassen 1990; O'Brien 1992; Hall 1993; Castells 1998) and to the agglomeration of company headquarters (Bosman and de Schmidt 1993) in core financial and administrative regions. In addition, many large urban areas also display considerable links between political and economic power (Rodríguez-Pose 1998: 81).

Agglomeration economies, i.e. localisation as well as urbanisation economies, play a central role in this process (e.g. Eberts and McMillen 1999; Sunley 2000). Economic agglomeration generates positive externalities which lower the production costs of one establishment as the output of others increases. The externalities result from businesses sharing non-excludable inputs, such as a large and proficient labour pool, technical expertise, communication and transportation networks, or a good infrastructural endowment, and from the untraded interdependencies emerging form the interaction of a large number of economic and social agents in a relatively small geographical area (Storper 1997). Financial and business service firms are considered a further major player fostering the concentration of economic activity in urban regions. These areas generally feature a strong link between advanced industries integrated in world economic circuits, on the one hand, and market-oriented services, on the other.

The urbanisation of capital and the rise of agglomeration economies are at the heart of a flourishing scholarly literature on world cities. Following Friedmann's (1986) seminal 'world city hypothesis' – which postulates the existence of a global hierarchy of cities developed as 'command and control centres' housing the headquarters of multinational corporations (MNC) – Sassen (1991) has highlighted that the key characteristic of world or global cities is their concentration of advanced producer services. Beaverstock et al. (1999) have resorted to Sassen's focus on producer services in order to classify cities as alpha, beta and gamma world cities based on the presence of accountancy, advertising, banking/finance and law firms.

World city studies have fundamentally dwelt on the attributes of particular cities. The relationships between cities have traditionally attracted somewhat less attention. Recently, however, there has been a shift in research focus towards the analysis of the expanding links between large urban areas (e.g. Taylor 2000, 2001 and 2003; Fosseart 2001; Taylor et al. 2002a) and methods to measure the extent of the global connectivity of leading cities across the world have been developed (e.g. Taylor et al. 2002b). Building upon Sassen's (1991) treatment of advanced producer firm services as producer of global cities, Taylor (2001) defines the world city network as an 'interlocking network'. From this perspective, world or global cities represent more than just international financial centres, they are

> "the locales for the production of knowledge-rich service products such as in inter-jurisdictional legal services, in place-sensitive international advertising campaigns, and in many new financial instruments" (Taylor 2003: 133).

Hence world cities are defined "in terms of the critical masses of creative and professional labour organised through global service firms" (ibid.), whose main role is to provide a flawless service for their clients by creating the connections between world cities through their office networks. Geographical distance plays a negligible role in this construct. Following Castells' (1996) network society approach, it is argued that the rise of new enabling technologies in computing and communication has allowed the overcoming of physical distance in the relationship between world cities.

Accordingly, many of the studies dealing with intercity relationships in a global world have tended to stress the interconnection among large urban areas to the detriment of their relationship with their immediate regional or national hinterland. Pierre Veltz's (1996, 2000) approach, for instance, proposes the progressive replacement of the links between urban centres and their immediate surrounding areas by

> "an 'archipelago economy' in which horizontal, frequently transnational, relations increasingly outmatch traditional vertical relations with the hinterland" (Veltz 2000: 33).

This metropolisation of the world economy is driven to a significant extent by the increasing importance of M&As. According to what has been outlined so far, large urban areas are perceived to be the perfect laboratories for interfirm relationships and for the completion of M&As, especially at a time when M&As have grown exponentially across the globe. M&As waves tend to be a cyclical phenomenon. Five waves of mergers have been identified during the 20th century by the literature on M&As, coinciding with periods of expansion in the world economy (e.g. Aliberti and Green 2000; Picot 2000). The last and most important wave in terms of overall volume took place during the 1990s and in particular during the second half of the decade. The total volume of cross-border M&As in the world increased more than six-fold during the 1990s (Rodríguez-Pose 2002: 25). In Germany the expansion was even greater. In 2000 the value of corporate transactions in Germany attained a volume of Euro 487 billion, compared to Euro 199 billion in 1999 or Euro 26 billion in 1990 (M&A 2001).

The reasons for the considerable increase of M&A activity are multiple and are addressed in the appropriate literature on foreign direct investment (FDI), though, at least for the time being, no unified theory of M&As or FDI exists (see Aliberti and Green 2000). Initial contributions to the theory of FDI, in general, and of mergers or acquisitions, in particular, have been put forward in Hymer's (1960) finance and portfolio theory, in Augmon's and Lessard's (1977) diversification theory of FDI, in Williamson's (1975, 1985) transactions cost economics and in Dunning's (1979) eclectic approach (or OLI-theory)^5. FDI can take a number of different forms, one of which includes the acquisition of a business enterprise or its assets. The multivariate and partly interrelated motives and theories which have been developed to explain these investment decisions are classified by Cooke (1988) as strategic (e.g. diversification, innovation, or efficiency), behavioural (i.e. interaction between the motives of management and the external environment) and economic (such as synergy, economies of scale, growth or multiple sourcing)^6.

The amount of literature focusing on the locational implications of M&As and on their impacts on economic development is, unfortunately, rather small. Initial attempts

---

[5] Dunning's (1979) eclectic theory states that a multinational enterprise will engage in FDI if the existience of ownership advantages, location-specific advantages and internalisation advantages are concurrently givien.

[6] Whereas a complete examination of FDI theories and approaches focusing the complexity of M&As lies beyond the scope of the compilation in hand, it is emphasised that considerable advances have been made in recent years, particularly with respect to the business and managerial factors behind M&As.

to investigate the relationship between economic integration, M&As and regional economic development have been undertaken by green 1990, Ashcroft and Love (1993) and Chapman and Edmond (2000). The latter authors, in their analysis of M&As in the EU chemical industry, observe that

> "[t]he shift in the motivation for and the general increase in the level of merger/acquisition activity is consistent with the a priori expectations regarding the effects of economic integration" (Chapman and Edmond 2000: 755).

Globalisation and economic integration thus affect the behaviour of firms – which had grown accustomed to local or nationally protected environments – in such a way that greater competition leads to moves by firms to secure and/or enhance their market share by means of a greater concentration of resources. This greater concentration of resources is basically achieved through M&As and the restructuring has important implications not just for the survival of the firm, but also for the economic weight of localities and regions. The consequences of a merger or an acquisition affect the product-mix, the production capacity and the various corporate functions between centres of activity. The impact of such changes upon places finds expression in the level and type of employment and affects inter-firm linkages and supply chains. Despite the fact that the geographical implications of these changes are not entirely clear, Chapman and Edmond (2000: 763) observe that M&As bring about changes in corporate control which, at the European scale, appear to favour the large urban areas of the northern 'core' countries, to the detriment of smaller urban areas within the core and of the southern 'periphery'. The consequences of the latest wave of M&As are hence likely to encourage the geographical concentration of high-level functions, a trend which is partly reflected in the increasing importance of international financial centres as the preferred location for corporate head-offices (see also Clark 1993).

The regional development implications of this phenomenon would depend on the degree to which the management of the enlarged enterprise permits the decentralisation of power and responsibility. Young et al. (1994) emphasise the existence of a permanent tension between centralizing and decentralizing tendencies within large companies and that the balance of these forces is crucial in assessing the consequences of M&A activity for regional economic development. However, this is an unequal battle. As the decision-making powers lie in the company headquarters, centralizing forces generally hold the upper hand. The consequence is that M&A transactions are therefore expected to trigger greater backwash than spread effects, fostering the concentration of management activities and economic development in large urban areas (Duranton and Puga 2001).

Does geographical distance play a role in determining the pattern of M&As? As already indicated, in the vast majority of theories dealing with the increasing concentration of economic activity, in general, and of the growing urbanisation of corporate control, in particular, geographical distance is regarded as almost irrelevant or merely attributed a minor role. In what is basically considered a space of flows, geographical distance is easily superseded by technological progress in telecommunications and by deregulation (O'Brien 1992, Castells 1996). Hence, M&As – as almost any other economic transaction – happen in a world which

> "is no longer well ordered by distance, clearly layered [...] between short- and long-span economies" (Veltz 2000: 38).

Even if this does not necessarily mean that the significance of distance disappears completely, "the territory that counts is more and more the territory of social interaction, not merely of physical proximity" (ibid.). From this perspective, the spatial pattern of M&As is governed by the interpersonal contacts of highly mobile and telecommunications-literate individuals, whose perception of distance is radically different from the simple geographical distance.

This supposed 'neutralisation' of distance stands, however, in sharp contrast with other recent research strands looking at the location of economic activity which have tended to stress the importance of physical proximity in determining the interaction between economic actors. One of these strands is the school of thought that emerged on the initial work of Paul Krugman, commonly referred to as 'geographical economics' (cf. Martin and Sunley 1996, for instance). Despite the fact that geographical economics have hardly been concerned with the individual behaviour of firms and regards individual companies as basically identical, this approach suggests that the agglomeration or dispersion of economic activity is governed by factors like transport costs, knowledge spillovers and labour market pooling effects (Krugman 1991; Venables 1998; Fujita et al. 1999), and all these factors are subject to significant distance decay effects (Fujita and Thisse 1996). As costs increase with distance, high transport costs in a geographical economics framework would favour the dispersion of economic activity, whereas a drop in transport costs will encourage agglomeration. The level of interaction between firms would thus be greatest, the lower the transportation costs and the lower the distance (Duranton and Puga 2000: 547).

Geographical economics also share with most strands dealing with innovation the idea that the transaction costs of the transmission of tacit knowledge and knowledge spillovers rise with distance (Audretsch and Feldman 1996, Narin et al. 1997), making the transmission of innovation across geographical distance costly and mainly achieved through pre-existent economic and research networks (Rodríguez-Pose 1999: 78). Finally the increasing importance accorded to transactions costs (Scott 1988) and untraded interdependencies (Storper 1997) implies that spatial proximity can lead to agglomeration economies and to significant cost reducing effects in the interaction among firms.

While, in many cases, the combination of transport and transaction costs, knowledge spillovers and untraded interdependencies leads – as in Castells' (1998) space of flows and similar approaches – to the agglomeration of economic activity in urban areas, the way of achieving this agglomeration varies significantly. Whereas Castells' framework agglomeration is the result of the interaction among firms sharing common functions, but often located in far away cities, in the approaches highlighting the role of transportation costs, spillovers and untraded interdependencies, agglomeration is achieved by the interaction of firms in nearby physical locations with the presence of a significant distance decay effect. When these theories are applied to the geography of M&As, this implies that in the former M&As are likely to be a fundamentally interurban phenomenon, in which the level of economic affinity and the networking between cities would play a much greater part than distance. In the latter, in contrast, interaction between firms is likely to take place within large urban agglomerations and to be significantly affected by geographical distance.

2.2 Territorial distribution and flows of M&As in Germany

The number of studies analysing whether M&As are basically a metropolitan phenomenon and whether the flows of M&As are affected by factors such as agglomeration and distance is, however, relatively small. This section tries to address these issues by looking at the dynamics of M&As[7] in Germany during the 1990s. Using the M&A Review database (made available by the University of St. Gallen and the *Institute for M&A* of University Witten-Herdecke and also found in the *Wirtschaftsdatenbank Gen-*

---

[7] From a business and economic perspective, mergers and acquisitions are distinguishable. In fact, the quantity of acquisitions involving the transfer of ultimate control from one company to another is far greater than the recorded total of mergers (Chapman and Edmond 2000). Spatially, in contrast, mergers and acquisitions are indistinguishable as both represent a process which transfers the corporate locus of control from the acquired firm to the acquiring one and possibly from one urban centre to another (Aliberti and Green 2000). For the purpose of this chapter, therefore, no distinction is made between mergers and acquisitions.

ios), which contains geographical information about ca. 29,900 M&As that took place in Germany between 1990 and 1999, the close to 24,600 cases in which both firms involved in the transaction were located in Germany are studied. Although the M&A Review database represents the most comprehensive record available for recent M&A activity in Germany, the dataset is not problemfree. The main shortcoming of the data source is that, although the geographical location of the firms involved in the transaction is recorded, precious few cases contain any detailed information about the size of firms or about the economic volume of the transaction. Hence, any research conducted using this database is necessarily limited to the number of M&As occurring in different locations, since reliable, consistent and comparable measures of the economic significance of different transactions are not always available.

With the intention of mapping the location of all M&As in Germany, postcodes were assigned to the headquarters of the firms involved in each individual transaction[8]; subsequently all M&As could have been allocated to the 40 German *Regierungsbezirke*), the administrative unit below the German *Länder*, according to where both the acquiring and the target firms where located. Given the theoretical discussion presented in the previous section, the hypotheses are:

> that the high levels of economic activity in large urban areas should be associated with high relative rates of M&As;
> that market size and economic agglomeration are likely to be important in this process, leading to an increasing concentration of economic activity in the largest German cities;
> that physical distance – as well as other factors such as the local endowment of human capital, the concentration of R&D activities and of political power – may also matter in the geography of M&As.

---

[8] German postcodes could not be given to every single merger or acquisition included in the database. Of the transactions, 6.5% of the transactions were lost as a result. The reasons for this loss range from those attributable to the way data was collected (i.e. errors associated to the manual entering of data in the database by Swiss students of University St. Gallen; the lack of postcode, according to the German postcode directory, for a limited number of locations included in the database; and the recording of same place in different ways in the database as, for example, Neustadt/Aisch vs. Neustadt a. d. Aisch) to external factors (i.e. several German locations have the exact same name and there are small differences between German and Swiss spelling. As most of these problems relate to very small locations and the attribution of postal codes to transactions taking place in urban agglomerations is generally straightforward, this has resulted in a slight overdimensioning of M&A events in urban regions.

The combination of these hypotheses implies that the wave of M&As in Germany during the 1990s would have led to the concentration of economic activity in large urban regions, with developed financial and/or real estate markets and a competitive socio-economic fabric. In the German context, this would mean that the large German metropoli hosting the main corporate and financial centres, such as Frankfurt, Dusseldorf, Munich, or Hamburg, as well as the top capital cities of the German *Länder* (*Landeshauptstädte*) would emerge as the winners from this process.

So as to test these hypotheses, an analysis is first conducted of the relative frequency of transactions by Regierungsbezirk, taking into account the size of the region in terms of population, total GDP and total number of firms. Then it is turned to the mapping of flows of M&A transactions from the main centres of economic activity. Finally, the factors behind the spatial pattern of M&A activity are studied by means of regression analyses, in which the number of M&As from each of the top German urban centres is regressed on a series of factors identified in the theoretical section.

2.2.1 Spatial distribution of M&As in Germany

With the purpose of an identification of the main centres of M&As in Germany, three locations quotients indicating the relative concentration of M&A activity per region have been estimated. The first index $MApR_{(comp)}\text{-}I$, represents an index of the M&As per region, standardized by number of companies in each region. It adopts the following formula:

$$MApR_{(comp)} - I = \frac{\sum_{t_0}^{t_1} MA_i \ / \ \sum_{t_0}^{t_1} C_i}{\sum_{t_0}^{t_1} MA_{Ger} \ / \ \sum_{t_0}^{t_1} C_{Ger}}$$

where MA depicts the absolute number of M&A transactions, C represents the total stock of taxable companies, t_0 and t_1 denote the period of analysis, i stands for the regional unit of analysis (Regierungsbezirk) and *Ger*, finally, corresponds to the whole of Germany. The two remaining indices $MApR_{(gdp)}\text{-}I$ and $MApR_{(pop)}\text{-}I$ take the total regional GDP and the population as the standardizing variable:

$$MApR_{(gdp)} - I = \frac{\sum_{t_0}^{t_1} MA_i \ / \ \sum_{t_0}^{t_1} GDP_i}{\sum_{t_0}^{t_1} MA_{Ger} \ / \ \sum_{t_0}^{t_1} GDP_{Ger}}$$

$$MApR_{(pop)} - I = \frac{\sum_{t0}^{t1} MA_i \; / \; \sum_{t0}^{t1} POP_i}{\sum_{t0}^{t1} MA_{Ger} \; / \; \sum_{t0}^{t1} POP_{Ger}}$$

GDP denotes the regional GDP (in million Euro) and POP the size of the population (in thousands). In all indices the German average is equal to 1.

Fig. 2.1 presents the results of the analysis[9]. The findings underline, as expected, that M&As are a fundamentally urban phenomenon, as shown by the strong concentration of M&As during the 1990s in the top German metropoli. Nine agglomerations perform above the German average in all three indices. These include Berlin, Bremen, Cologne, Dusseldorf, Frankfurt, Hamburg, Karlsruhe, Munich and Stuttgart. Alongside, Hanover scores above the German average when M&A activities are confronted with number of companies.

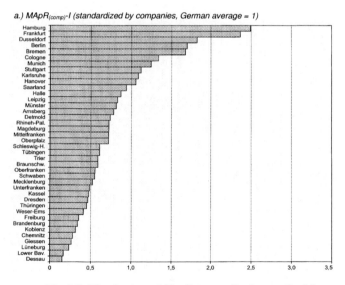

Fig. 2.1. Merging/acquiring firms per Regierungsbezirk

---

[9] For greater clarity, the names of the Regierungsbezirke of Darmstadt and Upper Bavaria have been substituted by that of their two main cities, Frankfurt and Munich respectively. In both cases, the principal city constitutes by far the main centre of M&As in the corresponding region.

2. M&A, Economic Development and Urban Regions

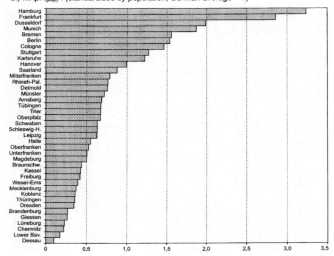

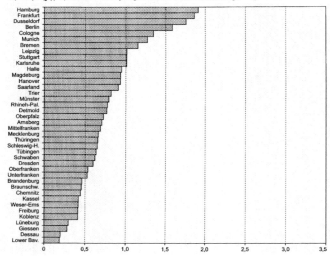

Fig. 2.1. Merging/acquiring firms per Regierungsbezirk (cont.)

None of the remaining thirty German *Regierungsbezirke* is above the German average in any of the indices. In the relatively rural regions which lack an articulating urban pole, such as Lower Bavaria, Lüneburg or Dessau, the incidence of M&As tends to be lower than one fifth of the German average.

There are, however, important differences in the relative occurrence of M&As among the top German metropoli. Frankfurt, Hamburg and Dusseldorf are by far the greatest poles of M&A activity. They appear as the top three agglomerations in all indices and Hamburg's and Frankfurt's scores are more than twice the German average when M&As are weighted by the number of companies (Fig. 2.1a) and the total GDP of the region (Fig.2.1c). Other large cities, such as Karlsruhe and Stuttgart, in contrast, barely exceed the German average in the three indices. That is, overall, six urban regions of prime importance and four subordinated ones come into view. Frankfurt, Hamburg and Dusseldorf are followed by the German capital, Berlin and by Munich and Cologne[10]. These six cities account for almost 55% of all M&As that took place in Germany between 1990 and 1999, and it is by no means a coincidence that precisely these six cities are regarded as the only German cities in the world city network (Taylor 2000: 10). If Bremen, Hanover, Karlsruhe and Stuttgart are included the percentage of German M&As concentrated in the top ten German cities increases to 69%.

An intra-regional analysis of M&As indicates an even greater concentration of economic activity. Most of the transactions take place within the municipal boundaries of the core city with a relatively small percentage in the regional hinterland. Even if Berlin, Bremen and Hamburg – where all M&As are concentrated in the city[11] – are not included, a strong agglomeration of M&A activities in core areas is evident. Munich hosts 82% of all M&As that take place in the *Regierungsbezirk* of Upper Bavaria, the city of Hanover 80% of those taking place in its region, and close to two thirds of the acquiring firms in the Darmstadt region are located in Frankfurt. The main exceptions to the rule are those regions where more than one key urban centre can be identified. This is the case of Dusseldorf (with secondary M&As centres in Essen and Duisburg), Cologne (Bonn) and Karlsruhe, where the main centre is located in Manheim. Nonetheless, the city of Cologne witnessed almost 50% and Dusseldorf nearly 40% of M&As in their respective region. In addition, there seems to be a strong distance decay effect, since neighbouring regions do not particularly benefit from their proximity to

---

[10] Bremen also scores well in two of the indices, although this results has to attributed rather to the relative low number of companies (Fig. 2.1a) and the small size of the market (i.e. population, Fig. 2.1b) in this city than to an extraordinary level of M&A activity.

[11] Berlin, Bremen, and Hamburg are city states consisting of only one municipality.

large agglomerations. The *Regierungsbezirke* of Giessen (next to Frankfurt), Lower-Bavaria (Munich), Brandenburg (Berlin), Freiburg (Stuttgart), Lüneburg (Hamburg), or Koblenz (located between Cologne and Frankfurt) are some of the regions with the lowest M&A indices.

In the light of these results, it could be claimed that M&As in Germany are not just an urban phenomenon, but one that is increasingly concentrated in large metropolitan areas With the exception of the period between 1990 and 1994, when firms in the *New Länder* of the former East Germany became the target of a flurry of acquisitions in the wake of German reunification (Zademach 2001), there has been a growing tendency for M&As to take place in the largest German metropoli. These results confirm those reached by other authors using case study analyses, which designate Frankfurt as the dominant centre for M&As in Germany with Dusseldorf, Munich, Berlin, Stuttgart and Cologne as additional centres (Lo 2000: 7n). Assuming that the merger of two companies and the acquisition of a company by another involve a shift in terms of decision-making structures, the results of the analysis corroborate the view that the recent wave of M&As in Germany is fostering a systematic concentration of corporate control in the main German metropoli.

2.2.2 Spaces of flows in the German market of M&A

The following section discusses in greater detail the dynamics of the concentration of firms and corporate control and decision-making structures in the six primary and four secondary centres of M&As in Germany. The flows of M&As in Germany in the 1990s have thereby been mapped, taking all the acquiring firms located in Frankfurt, Dusseldorf, Hamburg, Berlin, Munich and Cologne as well as Stuttgart, Hanover, Bremen and Karlsruhe as the starting point and analysing where the target firms are placed. The results of this exercise are presented in Fig. 2.2.

Three important findings emerge from the analysis. First and foremost is that a large proportion of M&As takes place within the same agglomeration. In the ten cases examined, the proportion of transactions in which the acquiring and the target firm are both located in the same region hovers between 20% and 30% of the total. This percentage is greater in Berlin, Hamburg and Munich, where the share of transactions taking place within the metropolitan area is close to 30%, and in Bremen, where it reaches 40%. Apart from Karlruhe (displaying with 17% the smallest proportion of intra-reginal M&As), in the remaining cities depicted in the series of maps, the share of intra-regional transactions is between 21 and 25%. If all M&As that took place in Germany between 1990 and 1999 are considered, the proportion rises slightly above 30% (Zademach 2001).

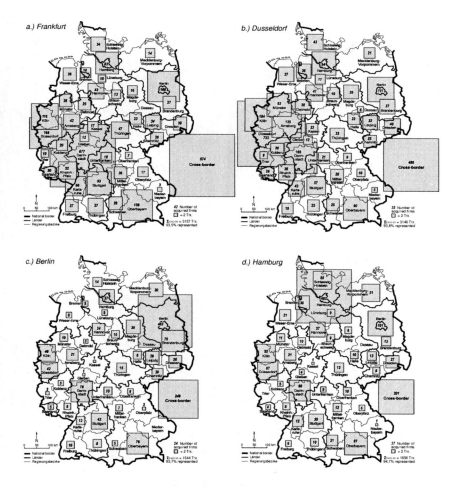

Fig. 2.2. Spatial distribution of M&A targets acquired from most important German metropoli

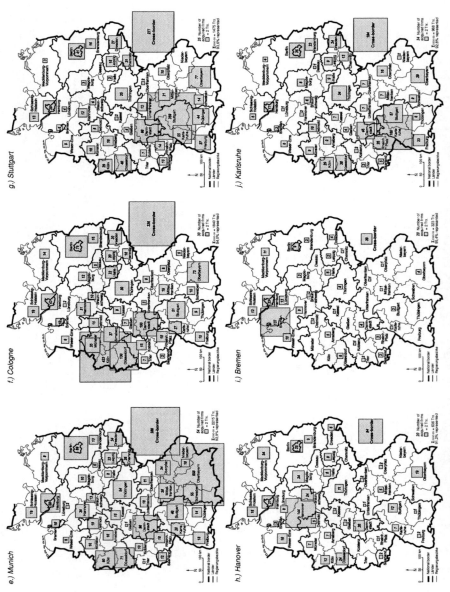

Fig. 2.4. Spatial distribution of M&A targets acquired from most important German metropoli (cont.)

A second factor emerging from Fig. 2.2 is the considerable degree of interconnectivity between the most important metropolitan areas. A significant share of all transactions takes place among the key German nodes of M&As. As a general rule, between 2% and 5% of the firms that have been acquired by local firms in the largest German M&As centres were located in another of the recorded large urban agglomerations. As a whole, the transactions involving just the six most important German M&A centres account for close to 50% of the overall level of M&As activity in each of these cities during the 1990s.

The final fact is the considerable and growing number of M&As involving German corporations where the target firm is foreign. Frankfurt has the greatest share of cross-border transactions, with more than one fifth of M&As involving foreign firms. In the remaining cities, with the exception of Bremen, the proportion of cross-border M&As is between 12% and 19% of the total. Cross-border M&As also became more important as the decade progressed. A sharp increase in the cross-border M&A activity can be reported in all cities depicted in the maps. In Frankfurt the proportion of cross-border transactions grew from levels of 19.4% in 1990, to over 24% in 1995 and 30.4% in 1999. In Berlin cross-border transactions represented 11.3% in 1990, 18.9% in 1995 and 32.6% at the end of the period of analysis. The German case confirms Chapman and Edmond's view for the whole of Europe that

> "[t]he number of cross-border deals has increased more rapidly than domestic transactions and there is no doubt that this activity has been at historically high levels over the last 10 years" (Chapman and Edmond 2000: 754).

In combination with the evidence from the previous section, Fig. 2.2 shows that the territorial distribution of M&As in Germany seem to be stressing the emergence of some of the features of an archipelago economy, in which corporate control becomes increasingly concentrated in a few key locations, whose economic connection with its immediate hinterland is rather limited. In order to assess whether this picture is entirely correct, it is now turned to the factors lying behind the identified patterns of M&As.

2.3 The factors shaping the geography of M&As in Germany

This section addresses the factors shaping the new geography of M&As in Germany in greater detail. In order to achieve this goal, first, the number of M&A transactions taking place in the core urban metropolitan areas are regressed on a set of independent variables which reflect the arguments outlined in the theoretical section.[12] This is followed by a stepwise multiple regression analysis in which the main indicators behind the flows of M&As in Germany are considered in conjunction.

2.3.1 Individual regressions: Agglomeration vs. proximity

Which factors explain the distinct concentration of corporate control in the most important German metropoli? In the theoretical section it was outlined that different strands of research have pointed out to diverse factors as the main drivers of the concentration of economic activity. Agglomeration, physical proximity, distance, the level of urbanisation, political power and a host of local characteristics were among elements highlighted by most approaches to the concentration of economic activity. In order to check the relevance of these factors, a series of indicators is constructed with the intention of testing their individual relationship to the number of M&As taking place from each of the main German urban regions. These indicators are introduced in the following model:

$$\ln MA_{itf\text{-}t0} = f\{samereg, neighreg, \ln dist, \ln GDP_{t0}, \ln GDP/cap_{t0},$$
$$\ln POP_{t0}, agriculture_{t0}, industry_{t0}, services_{t0},$$
$$education_{t0}, R\&D_{t0}, unemploy_{t0}, capital\}$$

in which the number of M&As (MA) taking place between region i and each of the remaining German regions (with the acquiring firm being located in region i) during the period of analysis t (1990-99) is a function of a series of indicators representing agglomeration, geographical distance and the socio-economic and political characteristics of individual regions.

The agglomeration independent variables include the dummy variable *samereg*, which controls for the fact, stressed in the previous section, that a large percentage of M&As take place within the same region. Other proxies for agglomeration include the total regional GDP (*GDP*) and the total population (*POP*) in 1990. Geographical distance is captured by two variables: *neighreg* is a dummy variable representing the *Bezirke* that share borders with the region being analysed, and *dist*, which depicts the

---

[12] Although it is appreciated that companies follow an economic, rather than a geographical, strategy when involved in an M&A activity in the first instance (cf. chapter 3.1. and 4.1.2 in more detail), operationalising purely corporate factors – such as shareholder activism, legal

geographical distance by the shortest road route between the main cities in the regions included in the analysis. Finally a series of other independent variables represent some of the basic characteristics of individual regions. The overall level of prosperity at the beginning of the period of analysis is captured by the initial GDP per capita (*GDP/cap*). The three variables *agriculture, industry* and *services* represent the respective proportion of employees in each sector at the beginning of the period. *Agriculture* also acts as a proxy for the degree of rurality of a region. *Education* stands for the share of the population with a university degree in 1995, *R&D* depicts the investment in R&D in % of regional GDP in 1996[13], *unemploy* stands for unemployment rate (in %) and *capital* is a trichotomous dummy variable, with the value of 0 given to regions that do not host the capital of the *Land*, 1 to regions where the *Landeshauptstadt* is located and 2 for the German capital, Berlin. This last variable represents a proxy for the concentration of political power.

Data in the analysis stem from the European Statistical Office (Eurostat) and from the German *Statistisches Bundesamt*. Natural logarithms for some of the independent variables (GDP, POP and GDP/cap), as well as for the dependent variable, are used in order to avoid problems of non-linearity. The regressions are conducted including all forty German regions with the *samereg* independent variable and excluding the region for which the analysis is taking place in all other cases. Tab. 2.1 presents the outcome of the univariate regressions in which the number of M&As conducted by firms located in Frankfurt, Dusseldorf, Berlin, Hamburg, Munich, Cologne, Stuttgart, Hanover, Bremen, or Karlsruhe between 1990 and 1999 was regressed on the independent variables for each of these cities.

The results of the individual regressions confirm the importance of intraregional transactions. In all cases, *samereg* has a positive and highly significant association with the number of M&As. The standardized β-coefficients always exceed 0.4 and reach 0.5 in the cases of Dusseldorf (0.513) and Bremen (0.558). This confirms the fact that firms searching for other firms to acquire or to merge with often tend to look for firms located in the same city and/or region.

In contrast to the positive and significant association between *samereg* and the number of M&As originating in the region of analysis, the variable representing

---

aspects or financial determinants – which vary distinctly from firm to firm is extremely problematic at this level of aggregation.

[13] Education data refer to 1995 and regional R&D investment to 1996, since no previous information was available at the regional level for the whole of post-1990 Germany.

neighbouring regions indicates that regional borders matter in the geography of German M&As. *Neighreg* tends to be not significant in most cases. These include Frankfurt, Hamburg, Munich, Cologne and Hanover and, to a lesser extent, Berlin. Dusseldorf represents the only exception to the rule among the top six German corporate centres with Bremen, Karlsruhe and Stuttgart also displaying positive and significant coefficients. In the case of Dusseldorf, the attraction of companies in neighbouring regions is possibly related to the location of some key economic centres, such as Bonn, Cologne, or Dortmund on its borders. Karlsruhe and Stuttgart are in a similar situation, since they both border the *Regierungsbezirk* of Darmstadt, the region where Frankfurt is located.

Tab. 2.1. M&As taking place from the six most important German metropoli regressed on the independent variables

a.) Frankfurt

Dependent Variable: ln MA_{iif-t0}					
	Variable	β (stand.)	t-statistic	R^2	df
samereg included	*samereg*	0.456***	3.113	0.209	1,38
without *samereg*	*neighreg*	- 0.009	- 0.053	0.000	1,37
	ln *dist*	- 0.069	- 0.419	0.005	1,37
	ln *GDP*	0.739***	6.678	0.547	1,37
	ln *GDP/cap.*	0.347**	2.252	0.121	1,37
	ln *POP*	0.782***	7.627	0.611	1,37
	% *agriculture*	- 0.609***	- 4.666	0.370	1,37
	% *industry*	- 0.185	- 1.145	0.034	1,37
	% *services*	0.433***	2.921	0.187	1,37
	Education	0.175	1.083	0.031	1,37
	investment in R&D	0.532***	3.817	0.283	1,37
	Unemployment	- 0.202	- 1.256	0.041	1,37
	capital city (political power)	0.476***	3.289	0.226	1,37

Note: ***, ** and * indicate significance at the 1, 5 and 10% level respectively

b.) Dusseldorf

Dependent Variable: ln MA_{iif-t0}					
	Variable	β (stand.)	t-statistic	R^2	df
samereg included	*samereg*	0.513***	3.682	0.263	1,38
without *samereg*	*neighreg*	0.497***	3.484	0.247	1,37
	ln *dist*	- 0.414***	- 2.766	0.171	1,37
	ln *GDP*	0.700***	5.966	0.490	1,37
	ln *GDP/cap.*	0.293*	1.863	0.086	1,37
	ln *POP*	0.793***	7.910	0.628	1,37
	% *agriculture*	- 0.621***	- 4.813	0.385	1,37
	% *industry*	- 0.304*	- 1.944	0.093	1,37
	% *services*	0.537***	3.876	0.289	1,37
	Education	0.222	1.382	0.049	1,37
	investment in R&D	0.402**	2.672	0.162	1,37
	unemployment	- 0.039	- 0.239	0.002	1,37
	capital city (political power)	0.456***	3.114	0.208	1,37

Tab. 2.1. M&As taking place from the six most important German metropoli regressed on the independent variables (cont.)

c.) Berlin

Dependent Variable: ln MA_{uf-t0}

	Variable	β (stand.)	t-statistic	R^2	df
samereg included	*samereg*	0.444***	3.056	0.197	1,38
without *samereg*	neighreg	0.274*	1.732	0.075	1,37
	ln dist	- 0.232	- 1.449	0.054	1,37
	ln GDP	0.442***	3.001	0.196	1,37
	ln GDP/cap.	- 0.045	- 0.272	0.002	1,37
	ln POP	0.724***	6.391	0.525	1,37
	% agriculture	- 0.278*	- 1.763	0.078	1,37
	% industry	- 0.180	- 1.114	0.032	1,37
	% services	0.288*	1.830	0.083	1,37
	education	0.492***	3.437	0.242	1,37
	investment in R&D	0.454***	3.103	0.206	1,37
	unemployment	0.137	0.843	0.019	1,37
	capital city (political power)	0.578***	4.312	0.334	1,37

d.) Hamburg

Dependent Variable: ln MA_{uf-t0}

	Variable	β (stand.)	t-statistic	R^2	df
samereg included	*samereg*	0.432***	2.955	0.187	1,38
without *samereg*	neighreg	0.115	0.703	0.013	1,37
	ln dist	- 0.264	- 1.662	0.069	1,37
	ln GDP	0.624***	4.855	0.389	1,37
	ln GDP/cap.	0.199	1.233	0.039	1,37
	ln POP	0.759***	7.087	0.576	1,37
	% agriculture	- 0.428***	- 2.883	0.183	1,37
	% industry	- 0.337**	- 2.178	0.114	1,37
	% services	0.507***	3.577	0.257	1,37
	education	0.278*	1.761	0.077	1,37
	investment in R&D	0.459***	3.144	0.211	1,37
	unemployment	0.005	0.029	0.000	1,37
	capital city (political power)	0.574***	4.265	0.330	1,37

Note: ***, ** and * indicate significance at the 1, 5 and 10% level respectively

e.) Munich

Dependent Variable: ln MA_{uf-t0}

	Variable	β (stand.)	t-statistic	R^2	df
samereg included	*samereg*	0.486***	3.432	0.237	1,38
without *samereg*	neighreg	0.176	1.090	0.031	1,37
	ln dist	- 0.184	- 1.141	0.034	1,37
	ln GDP	0.540***	3.907	0.292	1,37
	ln GDP/cap.	0.176	1.088	0.031	1,37
	ln POP	0.648***	5.177	0.420	1,37
	% agriculture	- 0.398**	- 2.642	0.159	1,37
	% industry	0.091	0.554	0.008	1,37
	% services	0.097	0.594	0.009	1,37
	education	0.256	1.608	0.065	1,37
	investment in R&D	0.380**	2.499	0.144	1,37
	unemployment	- 0.045	- 0.274	0.002	1,37
	capital city (political power)	0.407***	2.711	0.166	1,37

Tab. 2.1. M&As taking place from the six most important German metropoli regressed on the independent variables (cont.)

f.) Cologne

	Variable	β (stand.)	t-statistic	R^2	df
Dependent Variable: ln MA_{igf40}					
samereg included	*samereg*	0.480***	3.376	0.231	1,38
without *samereg*	*neighreg*	0.187	1.158	0.035	1,37
	ln *dist*	-0.235	-1.473	0.055	1,37
	ln *GDP*	0.586***	4.395	0.343	1,37
	ln *GDP/cap.*	0.150	0.925	0.023	1,37
	ln *POP*	0.754***	6.972	0.556	1,37
	% *agriculture*	-0.479***	-3.317	0.229	1,37
	% *industry*	-0.088	-0.535	0.008	1,37
	% *services*	0.287*	1.826	0.083	1,37
	education	0.367**	2.397	0.134	1,37
	investment in R&D	0.423***	2.841	0.179	1,37
	unemployment	0.045	0.272	0.002	1,37
	capital city (political power)	0.529***	3.792	0.280	1,37

g.) Stuttgart

	Variable	β (stand.)	t-statistic	R^2	df
Dependent Variable: ln MA_{igf40}					
samereg included	*samereg*	0.431***	2.948	0.186	1,38
without *samereg*	*neighreg*	0.326**	2.099	0.106	1,37
	ln *dist*	-0.321**	-2.062	0.103	1,37
	ln *GDP*	0.676***	5.579	0.457	1,37
	ln *GDP/cap.*	0.292*	1.855	0.085	1,37
	ln *POP*	0.745***	6.802	0.556	1,37
	% *agriculture*	-0.587***	-4.412	0.345	1,37
	% *industry*	0.007	0.041	0.000	1,37
	% *services*	0.254	1.599	0.065	1,37
	education	0.238	1.492	0.057	1,37
	investment in R&D	0.579***	4.320	0.335	1,37
	unemployment	-0.239	-1.494	0.057	1,37
	capital city (political power)	0.351**	2.283	0.123	1,37

Note: ***, ** and * indicate significance at the 1, 5 and 10% level respectively

h.) Hanover

	Variable	β (stand.)	t-statistic	R^2	df
Dependent Variable: ln MA_{igf40}					
samereg included	*samereg*	0.412***	2.791	0.170	1,38
without *samereg*	*neighreg*	0.177	1.093	0.031	1,37
	ln *dist*	-0.452***	-3.080	0.204	1,37
	ln *GDP*	0.406***	2.700	0.165	1,37
	ln *GDP/cap.*	0.007	0.045	0.000	1,37
	ln *POP*	0.610***	4.678	0.372	1,37
	% *agriculture*	-0.233	-1.457	0.054	1,37
	% *industry*	-0.436***	-2.950	0.190	1,37
	% *services*	0.489***	3.410	0.239	1,37
	education	0.375**	2.464	0.141	1,37
	investment in R&D	0.279*	1.765	0.078	1,37
	unemployment	0.268	1.691	0.072	1,37
	capital city (political power)	0.522***	3.723	0.273	1,37

Tab. 2.1. M&As taking place from the six most important German metropoli regressed on the independent variables (cont.)

i.) Bremen

	Variable	β (stand.)	t-statistic	R^2	df
Dependent Variable: ln MA_{tif-t0}					
samereg included	samereg	0.558***	4.148	0.312	1,38
without samereg	neighreg	0.437***	2.957	0.191	1,37
	ln dist	- 0.579***	- 4.316	0.335	1,37
	ln GDP	0.201	1.248	0.040	1,37
	ln GDP/cap.	- 0.025	- 0.153	0.001	1,37
	ln POP	0.342**	2.215	0.117	1,37
	% agriculture	- 0.112	- 0.684	0.012	1,37
	% industry	- 0.660***	- 5.340	0.435	1,37
	% services	0.643***	5.105	0.413	1,37
	education	0.252	1.585	0.064	1,37
	Investment in R&D	- 0.042	- 0.258	0.002	1,37
	unemployment	0.290*	1.843	0.084	1,37
	capital city (political power)	0.633***	4.976	0.401	1,37

j.) Karlsruhe

	Variable	β (stand.)	t-statistic	R^2	df
Dependent Variable: ln MA_{tif-t0}					
samereg included	samereg	0.408***	2.753	0.166	1,38
without samereg	neighreg	0.406***	2.699	0.165	1,37
	ln dist	- 0.262	- 1.653	0.069	1,37
	ln GDP	0.513	3.634	0.263	1,37
	ln GDP/cap.	0.112	0.683	0.012	1,37
	ln POP	0.672***	5.522	0.452	1,37
	% agriculture	- 0.373**	- 2.442	0.139	1,37
	% industry	0.144	0.886	0.021	1,37
	% services	0.035	0.212	0.001	1,37
	education	0.322**	2.072	0.104	1,37
	investment in R&D	0.523***	3.735	0.274	1,37
	unemployment	- 0.073	- 0.446	0.005	1,37
	capital city (political power)	0.426***	2.865	0.182	1,37

Note: ***, ** and * indicate significance at the 1, 5 and 10% level respectively

The lack of relevance of geographical proximity when considered as an individual variable in the spatial distribution of German M&As is reinforced when introducing the road distance between acquiring and target firm. As in the case of *neighreg*, *dist* is not robust in the majority of the top German M&As centres. No significant distance decay effect is observed in the M&As taking place form Frankfurt, Berlin, Hamburg, Munich, Cologne, or Hanover. Dusseldorf, Bremen, Karlsruhe and Stuttgart are again the exceptions. These results suggest that, as a general rule, geographical proximity and being close to one of the large metropolitan areas has little or no influence on the behaviour of firms when seeking for other firms to acquire or merge with. The main exception is being located in the same urban region, but in this case the significance of the results may be attributed to a series of factors related to economic agglomeration and clustering rather than simply to physical distance.

Economic agglomeration, in contrast, matters for M&As. The larger the size of the agglomeration in terms of total GDP or population plays an important part in determining where the target firms are located. Both the original GDP and population of the target firm's region are highly robust variables in explaining the choice of partners and targets by acquiring firms. The population of the target region is positive and highly significant in every single case. It is the strongest variable in all cases bar Bremen and explains, as a general rule, more than 50% of the variance. *GDP* is also positive and significant in all regressions, with the exception of Bremen and Karlsruhe (Tab. 2.1).

The association between the specific socio-economic features of individual regions and the flows of M&As in Germany varies across independent variables. With respect to the sectoral division of labour, whereas the share of employment in industry in the target regions generally bears no significant connection with M&As, employment in services and in agriculture are, for most cities, robust. Employment in services in the target region is positively associated with decisions to acquire or merge in the region of origin. The share of employment in agriculture – which can be interpreted as a proxy for rurality – shows the expected negative association with M&As. R&D investment has in all cases positive and significant coefficients. The overall level of education of the population of a target region is only positively connected to the number of M&As from Berlin, Hamburg, Cologne, Hanover and Karlsruhe, but not from the remaining cities.

The coefficients of the unemployment rates in target regions tend to be insignificant and vary sign across regressions. Likewise, regional GDP per capita lean towards being insignificant, with the exception of M&As taking place from Frankfurt and, to a lesser extent, from Dusseldorf and Stuttgart. Finally, the presence of a *Land* capital or of the federal capital, Berlin, in the target region – with its implications in the form of the concentration of political decision-making capacity – has a robust and positive connection with the number of M&As to that region from every single major M&A node in Germany.

This analysis of individual variables presents a panorama close to that pictured by Sassen, Taylor and Veltz. M&As in Germany during the 1990s seem to have led not just to a greater concentration of economic activity in the main urban metropoli, but also to a greater economic interaction among large urban centres, with neighbouring and rural regions playing almost no part in the process. Hence, the results seem to support, once again, the hypothesis of the emergence of an archipelago economy, in which management functions become more and more concentrated in a reduced number of core cities, with the traditional hinterlands playing progressively negligible roles.

2.3.2 Multiple regression analysis

Does this image of an archipelago economy hold, however, when instead of considering the relationship between dependent and independent variables individually, the interaction among independent determinants is taken into account in a multiple regression analysis? In this section, a stepwise multiple regression analysis is performed for the M&As performed from the same urban economic centres and including the same independent variables.

For various reasons, some variables have been taken out of this part of the analysis: *Samereg* has been excluded in order to prevent the distortion that the high percentage of intraregional M&As would provoke. As a consequence, the analysis only takes into account the M&As from one region to the remaining 39 German regions. The dummy for neighbouring regions (*neigh*) has been dropped, since the inclusion of the geographical distance between the main cities is a more accurate indicator of proximity. A strong level of multicollinearity between *POP* and *GDP* prevents the introduction of both variables together in regressions. *POP*, which is a more significant variable, has been chosen for the analysis, although the results of the analysis including *GDP* and *dist* are also reported. Since *agriculture* and *services* are in general two sides of the same coin, only the first variable is introduced in the model.

Accordingly, the model adopts the following form:

$$\ln MA_{ij\text{-}t0} = \alpha + \beta_1 \ln dist + \beta_2 \ln POP + \beta_3 \ln capital + \beta_4 agriculture + \beta_5 education + \beta_6 R\&D + \beta_7 unemploy + \varepsilon$$

Tab. 2.2 reports the results of the analysis for all M&As taking place from the six key German economic centres as well as, again, Bremen, Hanover, Karlsruhe and Stuttgart.

The results of the first two models, in which the number of M&As taking place from each city is regressed on distance as well as on one of the measures of agglomeration (POP in Model 1 and GDP in Model 2), first confirm the importance of agglomeration as a driver of M&As in Germany. The size of the target region, both in terms of population and total GDP, is an important explanatory factor in the geography of M&As.

However, the findings also reveal a much more complex role played by geographical distance than implied by the individual regressions. When considered in conjunction with population as an agglomeration indicator (Model 1), geographical distance becomes significant at the 1% level in all cases, except Frankfurt. The existence of a distance decay effect is also evident in connection to GDP as an agglomeration variable (Model 2), even though in this model the numbers of exceptions also include the main southern German nodes of Munich, Stuttgart and Karlsruhe. These results highlight that, once agglomeration is controlled for, firms searching for partners to merge with and for other firms to acquire tend to look in nearby rather than in distant locations.

Tab. 2.2. Explaining takeover activities in the German key nodes of M&A

a.) Frankfurt

Dependent Variable: $MA_{tgf\text{-}to}$	(1)	(2)	(3)	(4)	(5)
ln *dist*	-0.115	0.068	-0.212**	-0.092	-0.052
	(-1.122)	(0.600)	(-2.108)	(-0.961)	(-0.531)
ln *POP*	0.789***	-	0.685***	0.576***	0.475***
	(7.707)		(6.757)	(6.041)	(4.949)
ln *GDP*		0.752***	-	-	-
		(6.619)			
Capital city (political power)			0.297***	0.241**	0.211**
			(2.752)	(2.490)	(2.209)
% agriculture				-0.320***	-0.367***
				(-3.304)	(-3.456)
Education					0.318**
					(2.100)
Investment in R&D					0.001
					(0.011)
Unemployment					-0.304**
					(-2.239)
Constant	-6.535***	-7.103***	-4.209**	-3.462**	-3.108*
	(-3.643)	(-3.375)	(-2.271)	(-2.096)	(-2.015)
Observations	39	39	39	39	39
Degrees of freedom	2, 36	2, 36	3, 35	4, 34	7, 31
F-value	29.923	22.094	26.114	27.865	19.683
Significance (F)	0.000	0.000	0.000	0.000	0.000
R^2	0.624	0.551	0.691	0.766	0.816
Adj. R^2	0.604	0.526	0.665	0.739	0.775

Notes: t-statistics in parentheses; ***, ** and * indicate significance at the 1, 5 and 10% level respectively

Tab. 2.2. Explaining takeover activities in the German key nodes of M&A (cont.)

b.) Dusseldorf

Dependent Variable: MA_{itf-t0}	(1)	(2)	(3)	(4)	(5)
ln dist	-0.275***	-0.205*	-0.392***	-0.293***	-0.344***
	(-2.966)	(-1.687)	(-4.650)	(-3.598)	(-3.896)
ln POP	0.741***	-	0.596***	0.535***	0.504***
	(7.994)		(6.830)	(6.671)	(5.437)
ln GDP		0.633***	-	-	-
		(5.212)			
Capital city (political power)			0.343***	0.295***	0.225***
			(3.871)	(3.662)	(2.679)
% agriculture				-0.254***	-0.326***
				(-3.146)	(-3.580)
Education					0.227
					(1.607)
Investment in R&D					-0.086
					(-0.903)
Unemployment					-0.014
					(-0.117)
Constant	-3.168**	-1.552	-0.603	-0.351	-0.203
	(-2.106)	(-0.805)	(-0.419)	(-0.273)	(-0.143)
Observations	39	39	39	39	39
Degrees of freedom	2, 36	2, 36	3, 35	4, 34	7, 31
F-value	42.273	20.108	44.123	43.979	28.010
Significance (F)	0.000	0.000	0.000	0.000	0.000
R^2	0.701	0.528	0.791	0.838	0.863
Adj. R^2	0.685	0.501	0.773	0.819	0.833

c.) Berlin

Dependent Variable: MA_{itf-t0}	(1)	(2)	(3)	(4)	(5)
ln dist	-0.325***	-0.630***	-0.250**	-0.292***	-0.169
	(-3.182)	(-4.511)	(-2.616)	(-2.861)	(-1.151)
ln POP	0.764***	-	0.651***	0.613***	0.536***
	(7.472)		(6.527)	(5.862)	(5.194)
ln GDP		0.769***	-	-	-
		(5.505)			
Capital city (political power)			0.306***	0.297***	0.244**
			(3.029)	(2.946)	(2.568)
% agriculture				-0.120	-0.133
				(-1.141)	(-1.188)
Education					0.314*
					(2.005)
Investment in R&D					0.082
					(0.690)
Unemployment					-0.083
					(-0.522)
Constant	-6.988***	-1.995	-6.217	-4.835*	-6.741**
	(-3.483)	(-1.048)	(-3.399)	(-2.210)	(-2.236)
Observations	39	39	39	39	39
Degrees of freedom	2, 36	2, 36	3, 35	4, 34	7, 31
F-value	30.522	17.032	28.028	21.527	16.221
Significance (F)	0.000	0.000	0.000	0.000	0.000
R^2	0.629	0.486	0.706	0.717	0.786
Adj. R^2	0.608	0.458	0.681	0.684	0.737

Notes: t-statistics in parentheses; ***, ** and * indicate significance at the 1, 5 and 10% level respectively

Tab. 2.2. Explaining takeover activities in the German key nodes of M&A (cont.)

d.) Hamburg

Dependent Variable: MA_{if-t0}	(1)	(2)	(3)	(4)	(5)
ln dist	-0.207*	-0.261**	-0.182*	-0.182*	-0.220**
	(-2.000)	(-2.122)	(-1.941)	(-1.964)	(-2.170)
ln POP	0.743***	-	0.623***	0.567***	0.521***
	(7.194)		(6.126)	(5.193)	(4.292)
ln GDP		0.623***	-	-	-
		(5.070)			
Capital city (political power)			0.315***	0.305***	0.270**
			(2.994)	(3.023)	(2.403)
% agriculture				-0.134	-0.090
				(-1.324)	(-0.712)
Education					0.067
					(0.363)
Investment in R&D					0.153
					(1.117)
Unemployment					-0.046
					(-0.276)
Constant	-7.785***	-4.211*	-6.312***	-5.108**	-4.550*
	(-3.708)	(-1.868)	(-3.216)	(-2.382)	(-1.847)
Observations	39	39	39	39	39
Degrees of freedom	2, 36	2, 36	3, 35	4, 34	7, 31
F-value	29.154	15.155	26.721	20.910	12.357
Significance (F)	0.000	0.000	0.000	0.000	0.000
R^2	0.618	0.457	0.696	0.711	0.736
Adj. R^2	0.597	0.427	0.670	0.677	0.677

e.) Munich

Dependent Variable: MA_{if-t0}	(1)	(2)	(3)	(4)	(5)
ln dist	-0.315**	-0.211	-0.400***	-0.453***	-0.571***
	(-2.674)	(-1.555)	(-3.503)	(-4.083)	(-4.396)
ln POP	0.707***	-	0.607***	0.512***	0.544***
	(5.990)		(5.236)	(4.343)	(4.447)
ln GDP		0.551***	-	-	-
		(4.052)			
Capital city (political power)			0.315**	0.319***	0.208*
			(2.615)	(2.787)	(1.742)
% agriculture				-0.253**	-0.406***
				(2.210)	(-2.918)
Education					0.171
					(0.907)
Investment in R&D					-0.093
					(-0.685)
Unemployment					0.174
					(0.929)
Constant	-4.238**	-2.258	-2.129	0.234	0.115
	(-2.180)	(-1.001)	(-1.077)	(0.109)	(0.055)
Observations	39	39	39	39	39
Degrees of freedom	2, 36	2, 36	3, 35	4, 34	7, 31
F-value	19.203	9.131	17.158	15.517	10.600
Significance (F)	0.000	0.001	0.000	0.000	0.000
R^2	0.516	0.337	0.595	0.646	0.705
Adj. R^2	0.489	0.300	0.561	0.604	0.639

Notes: t-statistics in parentheses; ***, ** and * indicate significance at the 1, 5 and 10% level respectively

Tab. 2.2. Explaining takeover activities in the German key nodes of M&A (cont.)

f.) Cologne

Dependent Variable: $MA_{i,t-t0}$	(1)	(2)	(3)	(4)	(5)
ln *dist*	-0.308***	-0.341**	-0.385***	-0.351***	-0.443***
	(-3.064)	(-2.647)	(-3.858)	(-3.400)	(-4.842)
ln *POP*	0.664***	-	0.543***	0.511***	0.415***
	(6.610)		(5.072)	(4.656)	(4.036)
ln *GDP*		0.481***	-	-	-
		(3.737)			
Capital city (political power)			0.248**	0.232**	0.106
			(2.413)	(2.245)	(1.113)
% agriculture				-0.120	-0.193*
				(-1.181)	(-1.916)
Education					0.422***
					(2.846)
Investment in R&D					0.014
					(0.125)
Unemployment					-0.091
					(-0.715)
Constant	-5.316***	-1.660	-3.279*	-2.781	-2.602
	(-3.010)	(-0.788)	(-1.760)	(-1.463)	(-1.506)
Observations	39	39	39	39	39
Degrees of freedom	2, 36	2, 36	3, 35	4, 34	7, 31
F-value	36.572	16.282	29.502	22.717	20.838
Significance (F)	0.000	0.000	0.000	0.000	0.000
R^2	0.664	0.468	0.711	0.722	0.820
Adj. R^2	0.646	0.439	0.687	0.690	0.781

g.) Stuttgart

Dependent Variable: $MA_{i,t-t0}$	(1)	(2)	(3)	(4)	(5)
ln *dist*	-0.324***	-0.159	-0.394***	-0.357***	-0.315***
	(-3.338)	(-1.279)	(-4.025)	(-4.090)	(2.821)
ln *POP*	0.747***	-	0.663***	0.555***	0.481***
	(7.691)		(6.624)	(5.863)	(5.376)
ln *GDP*		0.635***	-	-	-
		(5.114)			
Capital city (political power)			0.229**	0.202**	0.079
			(2.173)	(2.165)	(0.897)
% agriculture				0.293***	-0.384***
				(-3.253)	(-3.963)
Education					0.409***
					(2.985)
Investment in R&D					-0.015
					(-0.141)
Unemployment					-0.178
					(-1.234)
Constant	-6.446***	-5.357**	-4.504**	-2.548	-3.242*
	(-3.347)	(-2.089)	(-2.208)	(-1.338)	(-1.897)
Observations	39	39	39	39	39
Degrees of freedom	2, 36	2, 36	3, 35	4, 34	7, 31
F-value	35.049	16.647	27.356	28.783	23.847
Significance (F)	0.000	0.000	0.000	0.000	0.000
R^2	0.661	0.480	0.701	0.772	0.843
Adj. R^2	0.642	0.452	0.675	0.745	0.808

Notes: t-statistics in parentheses; ***, ** and * indicate significance at the 1, 5 and 10% level respectively

Tab. 2.2. Explaining takeover activities in the German key nodes of M&A (cont.)

h.) Hanover

Dependent Variable: MA_{iif-t0}	(1)	(2)	(3)	(4)	(5)
ln *dist*	-0.486***	-0.511***	-0.477***	-0.490***	-0.545***
	(-4.647)	(-3.998)	(-5.092)	(-5.182)	(-4.423)
ln *POP*	0.636***	-	0.511***	0.552***	0.499***
	(6.079)		(5.029)	(5.035)	(4.163)
ln *GDP*		0.470***	-	-	-
		(3.678)			
Capital city (political power)			0.320***	0.323***	0.276**
			(3.153)	(3.181)	(2.370)
% agriculture				0.103	0.093
				(0.999)	(0.737)
Education					0.211
					(1.114)
Investment in R&D					0.036
					(0.266)
Unemployment					-0.136
					(-0.705)
Constant	-2.828	0.936	-1.202	-1.904	-1.170
	(-1.371)	(0.413)	(-0.627)	(-0.933)	(-0.446)
Observations	39	39	39	39	39
Degrees of freedom	2, 36	2, 36	3, 35	4, 34	7, 31
F-value	27.826	13.114	26.473	20.103	11.715
Significance (F)	0.000	0.000	0.000	0.000	0.000
R^2	0.607	0.421	0.694	0.703	0.726
Adj. R^2	0.585	0.389	0.668	0.668	0.664

i.) Bremen

Dependent Variable: MA_{iif-t0}	(1)	(2)	(3)	(4)	(5)
ln *dist*	-0.545***	-0.569***	-0.567***	-0.566***	-0.590***
	(-4.230)	(-4.276)	(-6.285)	(-6.192)	(-5.136)
ln *POP*	0.277**	-	-0.017	-0.009	-0.026
	(2.145)		(-0.164)	(-0.077)	(-0.197)
ln *GDP*		0.170	-	-	-
		(1.275)			
Capital city (political power)			0.628***	0.627***	0.629***
			(6.222)	(6.107)	(5.146)
% agriculture				0.015	0.004
				(0.140)	(0.029)
Education					0.095
					(0.480)
Investment in R&D					-0.049
					(-0.334)
Unemployment					-0.112
					(-0.632)
Constant	2.093	4.063**	5.786***	5.659***	6.031**
	(0.952)	(2.026)	(3.511)	(2.975)	(2.607)
Observations	39	39	39	39	39
Degrees of freedom	2, 36	2, 36	3, 35	4, 34	7, 31
F-value	12.521	10.284	29.999	21.874	11.609
Significance (F)	0.000	0.000	0.000	0.000	0.000
R^2	0.410	0.364	0.720	0.720	0.724
Adj. R^2	0.377	0.328	0.696	0.687	0.662

Notes: t-statistics in parentheses; ***, ** and * indicate significance at the 1, 5 and 10% level respectively

Tab. 2.2. Explaining takeover activities in the German key nodes of M&A (cont.)
j.) Karlsruhe

Dependent Variable: MA_{if-it}	(1)	(2)	(3)	(4)	(5)
ln *dist*	-0.229*	-0.109	-0.269**	-0.258**	-0.348**
	(-1.949)	(-0.730)	(-2.321)	(2.154)	(-2.246)
ln *POP*	0.661***	-	0.562***	0.543***	0.520***
	(5.622)		(4.478)	(4.045)	(3.774)
ln *GDP*		0.478***	-	-	-
		(3.188)			
Capital city (political power)			0.235*	0.228*	0.078
			(1.851)	(1.767)	(0.582)
% agriculture				-0.058	-0.112
				(-0.451)	(-0.787)
Education					0.277
					(1.355)
Investment in R&D					0.074
					(0.463)
Unemployment					0.067
					(0.326)
Constant	-4.889**	-2.814	-3.293	-3.024	-3.291
	(-2.344)	(-1.012)	(1.500)	(-1.316)	(-1.507)
Observations	39	39	39	39	39
Degrees of freedom	2, 36	2, 36	3, 35	4, 34	7, 31
F-value	18.301	6.784	14.166	10.433	7.831
Significance (F)	0.000	0.003	0.000	0.000	0.000
R^2	0.504	0.274	0.548	0.551	0.639
Adj. R^2	0.477	0.233	0.510	0.498	0.557

Notes: t-statistics in parentheses; ***, ** and * indicate significance at the 1, 5 and 10% level respectively

Hence, in combination with agglomeration, M&A activity increases with spatial proximity. This finding introduces important nuances in the perception of the panorama of M&As as an archipelago economy and brings the geography of German M&As closer to the strands of economic geographers such as Storper or geographical economists like Krugman who emphasize that, despite the fact that agglomeration may be considered as one of the most important factor shaping economic activity, distance decay effects can be identified in economic relationships.

The proxy for political power (*capital*) in the third model is robustly associated with the number of M&As between any two regions. This implies that firms not only tend to look for firms to acquire or merge within large urban and not too distant areas, but also preferably in those regions where economic and political powers concur.

The introduction of socio-economic variables in Models 4 and 5 does not significantly alter the results. Employment in agriculture, for example – which was in most cases significant in the individual regressions – becomes a less important factor in target regions. When considered in combination with other variables, the level of employment in agriculture and the rurality of a region turn out as insignificant elements in the M&As taking place from Berlin, Hamburg, Cologne, Bremen or Karlsruhe. Only M&As originated in Frankfurt, Dusseldorf, Munich and Stuttgart seem to be affected by the sectoral specialisation of the target region. Smiliarly, the rate of unemployment rate does not display a significant association in nine out of the ten cases considered. The endowment of human capital in target regions is only significant in three out of ten, with Berlin as a borderline case. But the most remarkable change with respect to the individual regressions is the robustness of investment in R&D. This variable was positively associated with the number of M&As and significant in almost every single individual regression presented in the previous section. Yet, when considered in conjunction with other factors the technology effort of target regions becomes irrelevant for companies looking for a firm to acquire or merge with in other regions in every single one of the regressions.

The loss of significance of many of the variables representing the socio-economic characteristics with respect to the simple regression analysis implies that, given the robustness of the agglomeration indicators, factors such as the educational endowment of the population or the specialisation in R&D, as well as many other regional characteristics, seem to be encompassed in the level of agglomeration of the target region.

As a whole, the geography of M&As in Germany during the 1990s is basically explained by the combination of agglomeration, distance and political power of Model 3. The three variables included in this model explain in all cases two thirds of the variance in the dependent variable. The introduction of additional variables in Models 4 or 5 does not significantly increase the explanatory capacity of the model. The only exception is related to the M&As taking place from Frankfurt, the economic centre that exhibits the highest level of openness as the national economic and financial centre (Wójcik 2002: 886). In this case variables such as the level of employment in agriculture, the human capital and the rate of unemployment of target regions are robust and to a certain extent cover for the lack of significance of geographical distance.

2.4 Conclusions

The aim of this chapter has been to study the geography of corporate takover and mergers in Germany during the 1990s and to unravel the factors behind its territorial distribution. In contrast to the huge body of literature focusing on economically driven strategies at the level of the firm, this analysis has dealt with the spatial determination of M&A activity.

Three main conclusions can be extracted from the analysis. The first conclusion is that M&As are fundamentally a large city phenomenon and, thus, are causal to the economic take-off of the main German metropoli. Regardless of how the geographical incidence of takeovers is measured, the results show that the transactions taking place in the largest German cities far outweigh in relative terms all those taking place in other regions. The wave of M&As of the 1990s has hence contributed to a major concentration of firms, company headquarters, and economic activity in the key Germany metropoli.

Secondly, it has been stressed that a large percentage of all transactions take place within the same region or involves companies already located in large urban centres, a factor that concurs with the large body of literature emphasizing the relevance of inter-city relationships in a increasingly globalising world. There is also evidence that the number of cross-border transactions grew as the 1990s progressed and is particularly important for the main economic centres in Germany, and especially for Frankfurt.

Thirdly, the results show that factors such as economic agglomeration and the concentration of political power are the main drivers behind the flows of M&As. Although many local socio-economic characteristics are associated with the geography of mergers and takeovers when considered individually, their effect seems to be encompassed by the inter-relationship between economic and social factors in large cities, when analysed in conjunction with agglomeration indicators. In contrast, geographical distance – which as an individual variable has a negligible role in the geography of M&As – becomes significant in combination with agglomeration indicators. Even if German firms seek for targets primarily in other German large urban areas, there is a greater chance they would look for them in neighbouring rather than in far away urban regions.

The analysis has presented a general overview of the geography of M&As in Germany, but, in many ways, it also suggests that further research is needed in order to fully understand the conditions that have driven the recent wave of takover activities. With regard to the dynamics of corporate takeovers, many questions remain unanswered; future investigations may address, for instance, the changing hierarchy of M&A nodes or the evolution of the importance of factors such as distance and agglomeration on takeovers. Studies by sector and industry are required in order to identify different patterns across industries and, when adequate data become available, some of the questions presented in this chapter will have to be revisited in order to analyse the geographical impact of M&As on employment and regional GDP. But perhaps the greatest need is for specific case studies examining in detail M&A transactions within and across urban areas in order to untangle in which way the factors and the dynamics taking place within large urban agglomerations become a magnet for corporate merger and takover activities not only in Germany, but also possibly across the globe.

3 GEOGRAPHICAL DYNAMICS IN THE OLD AND NEW ECONOMY – THE MARKETS OF M&A IN GERMANY[14]

Since the mid 1980s most of Europe and the developed world experienced an unprecedented wave of mergers and acquisitions (M&As) that only faded away during the economic downturn at the beginning of the 21st century. In 2000 the global market for M&As represented US$ 3,498 billion[15] (UN 2002). Germany, together with the US and the UK, was one of the three most important markets for M&As (Economic Intelligence Unit 1996; Kang and Johansson 2000). During the 1990s alone, around 30,000 corporate takeovers involved at least one German firm.

This massive number of takeovers has led to important changes not just in the structure of businesses, but also to a thorough reshuffling in the location of economic activity and decision-making. In Germany and elsewhere M&As have contributed to an increasing concentration of firms and corporate control in core regions and urban agglomerations, and to the reinforcement of existing headquarter locations as major economic control nodes (Ò hUhallachàin 1994; Green and Mayer 1997; Chapman and Edmond 2000; see also Duranton and Puga, 2003). Yet whereas research on corporate takeovers from a microeconomic perspective is extensive, the number of empirical studies examining its overall effects on the location of economic activity is still relatively small. In particular the relevance of place-specific attributes in M&A decisions remains a deeply neglected topic in economic geographical research.

This chapter builds on the exploration of the impact of the wave of M&As in the 1990s on the changing geography of economic activity in Germany provided in the previous sections. Its aim is to deepen the understanding of the role played by location factors in M&A activity, paying particular attention to a dynamic examination of the

---

[14] This chapter represents the result of research conducted as visiting doctoral student at the London School of Economics in autumn 2003. Helpful comments from Andrés Rodríguez-Pose as well as the participants of the 66. *Wissenschaftliche Jahrestagung des Verbandes der Hochschullehrer für Betriebswirtschaft e.V.* in Graz, June 2004 as well as Hans-Dieter Haas and Arnold Picot on an earlier draft (the author's *Projektstudie* in his postgradual study programme *Betriebswirtschaftliche Forschung*) are greatly acknowledged.

[15] After 2000 the volume of transactions quickly waned to US$ 1,753 billion in 2001 and to US$ 1,230 billion in 2002 (UN 2003; Thomson Financial 2003).

changes in the spatial distribution of M&As across ten German industrial sectors, which range from knowledge intensive, so-called 'new economy' industries such as financial services, media or information and communication technologies (ICT) to more traditional 'old' sectors like automotive, heavy manufacturing, or the textile industry.

Taking, again, the M&A Review database of the German Handelsblatt group as the source of data, German M&As during the 1990s are examined in order to identify different types of processes and their spatial impact across sectors. First, attention is paid on the possible existence and significance of local clustering processes, i.e. *economies of proximity and agglomeration*, and the *degree of metropolitan interconnectivity* (or 'archipelago economies'). Second, the gravitational forces of different industrial sectors are scrutinized, highlighting whether there is a *tendency towards concentration* of economic activity in large agglomerations. Finally the changing role of *geographical distance* and its effect on M&As is studied. As will be demonstrated, these four determinants significantly shaped the geography of M&As in Germany and enable valuable insights on the sector specific characteristics and dynamics of corporate takeovers.

This chapter is divided into four further sections. By reviewing the notwithstanding its recent growth still rather scarce literature addressing M&As from an spatial respectively aggregated point of view, the next sections provides some basic reflections on the key reasons underlying M&As and its implications, as well as a specific economic geographical conceptualisation of corporate takeovers as relational processes. After a brief description of the database and the applied methodology, section 3.2 reports the results of the empirical analysis focusing the territorial dynamics of the wave of M&As in Germany. In section 3.3, these territorial dynamics are examined in five sectors of the 'new' ecomomy (financial services, insurance, transport, media, and IC/CT) and five 'old' economy industries (heavy manufacturing, automotive, energy, chemicals, and textiles). Section 3.4 finally presents concluding remarks.

3.1 Corporate takeovers in spatial perspective

As the today's dominant form of foreign direct investment in developed countries, M&As have become one of the main drivers of industrial restructurung. Although M&As – representing the most permanent and constraining end of a spectrum of formal relationships between firms, including strategic alliances and joint ventures – are often bundled together for research purposes, there are important differences between a merger and an acquisition. A merger implies the combination of the assets and operations of two firms to establish a new entity whose control resides in a team from one or both of the two. Acquisitions (or takeovers), on the other hand, indicate the purchase of a company by transferring the control of assets and operations from one firm to the other, the former becoming an affiliate of the acquirer. In M&A transactions, acquisitions are far more common than mergers: 97% of all cross-border M&As reported in the World Development Report were defined as acquisitions (UN 2000).[16]

3.1.1 Key factors underlying the most recent wave of M&As

Firms engage in M&As activity for several reasons. The basic strategic corporate objectives include the search for new markets, increased market power and dominance, greater size and scope, efficiency gains through synergies, and geographic and product line diversification, i.e. the spreading of risk. Corporate takeovers enable firms to quickly access strategic proprietary assets, such as skilled labour, patents, brands, licenses, or management skills (Porter 1990; Trautwein 1990; Berkovitch and Narayanan 1993; Dunning 1997). Further central factors motivating firms to undertake M&As are financial enticements, like tax treatment and subsidies, transfer pricing, trade barriers, transportation costs, or monopoly type practices (Ravenscraft and Scherer 1987; Healy et al. 1992; Loughran and Vij 1997; compare also Clark 1993; Wrigley 1999) and personal, so behavioural attributes (Shleifer and Vishny 1989; Avery et al. 1998; Shinn 1999). The central rationale behind M&As is thus one of achieving greater efficiency.

The most recent wave of corporate consolidation, however, also relates to the principal changes in the global economic environment, most notably the processes of political transformation and integration (addressed in more detail in chapter 4), as well as the global tendency towards privatisation, liberalisation, and deregulation (UN 2000). Additional dynamic and interacting drivers leading to greater competition and restructuring are technological innovation, improved access to international financial markets, as well as new, globally networked modes of production (Henderson et al. 2002). The various basic factors motivating firms to undertake M&As combine with the op-

---

[16] Due to the lack of reliable data on this issue for Germany, no distinction is made between mergers and acquisitions in this chapter, although, given international trends, it could be assumed that the great majority of transactions are in fact acquisitions or corporate takeovers.

portunities and pressures of the increasing globalisation of markets and drive firms to pursue their overarching strategic goal: to defend and develop their competitive markets. In particular as sanctions, like being taken over or strategic disadvantages consequential to merging rivals, await those who fail to deliver growth and profits, survival in an increasingly competitive environment is therefore the overall strategic driver of M&As (UNCTAD 2000).

Whereas financial economists concentrate on efficiency gains and – particularly if operant as service provider in M&A business – generally welcome merger waves (compare Gerke at al. 1995; Boehmer and Loeffler 1999), industrial economist and antitrust divisions or cartel commissions tend to assess M&A activity in a rather suspicious manner (Bundeskartellamt 2001; Gugler et al. 2003; Monopolkommission 2003). But apart from the well established effects corporate takeovers have on economic change (e.g. Curry and George 1983; Jensen and Ruback 1983; Davies and Lyons 1996; Nilsson and Schamp 1996), corporate takeovers also imply profound political and socio-institutional implications and are by no means an 'aspatial phenomenon': Strategic decisions on the transfer of assets and control affect not only the firms involved, but also both the locations and metropolitan systems with which they are associated and the organisational and geographical shape of industries as a whole. In brief, M&As have become one of the keys in shaping the location of economic activity and decision-making.

3.1.2 Spatial and developmental implications of M&As: On corporate control and metropolitan systems

Corporate takeovers allow firms to acquire rapidly a portfolio of locational assets, i.e. knowledge, ideas, or processes of interactive learning specific to a certain locality. Suchlike 'localised capabilities' (Maskell and Malmberg 1999) have become key sources of competition strength in the globalising economy (as will be discussed in more detail in chapter 4). As M&As do however not necessarily add productive assets or new jobs to a locality, their developmental impacts are controversially discussed. Compared to greenfield investments, i.e. the setting up of new affiliates, takeovers or mergers are less likely to transfer new or better technologies or skills, since the financial resources provided through corporate takeovers do not always add to the local capital stock. They also may lead to employment loss due to downgrading or closure of local production or functional activities (e.g. R&D), their relocation in line with the acquirer's corporate strategy, or the breaking up of the acquired firm and divestment of its individual parts. Furthermore, M&As can be used to reduce competition, strengthen market power and thus lead to anti-competitive results.

On the other side, when helping to preserve local firms that might otherwise would have gone under, corporate takeovers may prevent concentration from increasing. And as takeovers are often followed by sequential investments by the acquirer, in the long term, M&As also can lead to enhanced investment in production. Similarly, they can involve transfers of new and improved technologies and increase the operational efficiency of the targets. Especially in times of intense competitive pressures or overcapacity in global markets, corporate reorganisation through an M&A transaction may be beneficial; the advantage of takeovers or mergers in such conditions is that they rapidly restructure existing capacities that would have otherwise risked downsizing or closure (UN 2000).

If considered in their totality, the spatial distribution of M&As intensely affects the overall organisation of an economy through modifications in regional and urban structures: The changing ownership structure and the resulting transfer of the corporate locus of control as well as the shifting of assets and personal across geographic areas and industries adversely impacts on the localities involved. M&As thus cause fundamental alterations in corporate space and increase the risk of external domination of segments of a local economy. Companies and establishments at peripheral regions, for instance, have become increasingly owned and controlled by companies headquarted in core regions (Chapman and Edmond 2000).

As decisions made in the highest level of corporate control directly influence the growth and development of city systems, the performance of major corporations has firsthand impacts on interrelationships in a nation's urban structure (Green 1990). M&A activity has thus to be conceived as a paramount driver for the particular role of cities as increasing concentrated locations of power and control, as principally conceptualised by Friedman (1986), Sassen (1991, 2000), Castells (1996), Taylor (2000), Duranton and Puga (2003) and others in the theory on globalized urban networks. In extension of the contemplations of these scholars, Veltz (1996, 2000) argues that the functional links between cities with similar role in a world economy are strengthened beyond physical contiguity; in his 'archipelago economy' approach, he proposes that the connections between cities are greatly enhanced, whereas they become progressively more detached from their regional contexts and hinterlands (compare section 2.2). Representing important stationary relocation processes that permit the transfer or corporate power from one metropolitan complex to another (Green 1990: 8), corporate takeovers strengthen the increased interconnectivity between large urban areas.

In sum, M&As reinforce the spatial concentration of economic activity, the resulting disparities in regional development, and the changes and linkages in an economy's metropolitan hierarchy. Hence, the concentration of power and control resulting from M&A activity has implications for regional development and indicates the importance of corporate strategy and the spatial organisation of production to metropolitan systems.

3.1.3 Takeovers and mergers on the academic research agenda

Despite this relevance, comprehensive and, most notably, comparative empirical studies addressing the spatial impact of corporate takeovers – be it at aggregate, industry, or firm level – remain scarce (e.g. Markusen 2001). The main reason behind the relative neglect of the importance of M&As in geographical location analyses has traditionally been limited data availability (Sachwald 1994, Chapman and Edmond 2000, see also chapter 2). Until recently the data sets on M&As were scarce and/or unreliable. Indeed, over the last few years corporate data sets have improved and the study of M&As has become more popular within economic geography.

A great majority of recent studies, however, focuses on one explicit industry (e.g. Ashcroft and Love 1993; Lagendijk 1995; Nuhn 1999a, 2004; Chapman and Edmond 2000; Lo 2000; cf. also Lo 2003), or studies single cases of firms or M&A transactions (e.g. Bathelt and Griebel 2001; Nuhn 1999b, 2001; Zeller 2000; for a more comprehensive literature review, see Green and Mayer 1997). Though this type of research has delivered inspiring theories and empirical evidence abouth the motives driving M&As and about post-mrger od acquisitions restructuring processes, they unfortunately offer very little on the role played by location attributes in takeover activity, the extent to which place-specific advantages concern merger decisions, how M&As affect economic location and, most notably, how sectoral specifics relate to more general M&A patterns.[17]

Industry characteristics, such as growth prospects, market structure and competition have, nevertheless, a strong influence on corporate takeovers (Kang and Johansson 2000: 30). This becomes manifest when the *a priori* distinct locational patterns of

---

[17] Though a small number of exceptions exists (e.g. Lorenzen and Mahnke 2002), this observation largely applies to organisational studies beyond the economic geographical literature, too.

'old' (i.e. primarily manufacturing) industries, and the "globalised, information-based socio-economic formation" (Martin 2002) of the new economy are compared.

3.1.4 Differing location specifics in differing economies

Based around a particular technology, the one of the Internet, the new economy is characterized by dynamic markets, networked organisation forms, and digitisation as key technological drivers (Kelly 1998; Gillespie et al. 2001; Martin et al. 2003). In essence, its industries are specialised in the provision of immaterial intellectual outputs, that can be transported online virtually without costs. New economy sectors fundamentally depend on processes of knowledge creation, interactive learning, and innovation, in which human and social capital, R&D activity and the attraction of talent in places rich in ideas are key determinants for success. A new entrepreneurial culture, networks of interaction, collaboration, flexibility as well as broad skills and the adaptability to innovate became more relevant corporate strategic assets than the physical location associated with the transport of raw materials to the producer and goods to the market. In order to survive and progress, new economy companies are often compelled to look for partners from whom such intangible assets can be obtained and absorbed.

'Old' economy manufacturing firms, in contrast, still rely on material goods, economies of scale, exports, and physical capital as the main sources of value. The dominant technological mode of mature industrial sectors is mechanisation; job specific skills are therefore more important than broad skills, flexibility and adaptability, and R&D activities are of rather low or moderate importance. Although traditional sectors increasingly use new economy technologies such as ICT, costs and availability of labour and real estate, provision of space, access to road networks, and transport infrastructure, as well as proximity to markets, are still the key determinants in their location decisions.

These very diverse forms of industrial organisation can be expected to generate different location patterns. Traditional activities, given their need for extensive spaces, would look, following a Weberian tradition, for proximity to markets, raw materials, energy and labour, with transport costs having a capital role in their ultimate location. The restructuring of these activities through M&As is unlikely to alter their established territorial pattern. Knowledge-intensive sectors and related industries, in contrast, rely significantly on the distance-transcending capabilities of new technologies. In theory, this allows for much greater flexibility in terms of location, with economic activity capable of emerging almost anywhere. Such a "weightless economy" (Quah 1996, 1997; Coyle 1997) and the "death of distance" (Cairncross 1997) that, in theory, characterises these sectors can result in a much greater dispersal of economic decision-making.

Many of the characteristics of the knowledge-intensive sectors point, however, in an opposite direction. According to Leamer and Storper (2001), the new economy – while permitting a decentralisation of certain routinised activities – will participate in reinforcing the need for urban concentration and agglomeration. Economic success in the knowledge-intensive services often hinges on the creation of networks, on social interaction, locally based tacit knowledge, and personal contacts – factors whose genesis is significantly facilitated by geographical proximity. The emergence of strong clustering effects such as the concentration of 'dot.com' start-ups or multimedia industries in major cities such as London, New York, or Los Angeles is one spatial expression of the new economy (e.g. Scott 1996; Pratt 2000; Grabher 2001, 2002; Florida 2002; compare also Martin and Sunley 2003). Several of the essential factors in these sectors are, in turn, central dimensions in M&A activity as well. Under these circumstances, M&As in less traditional and mature sectors could reinforce the agglomeration of economic decision-making, perpetuating core-periphery patterns.

3.1.5 Corporate takeovers and economic geography – a relational perception

The distinctly varying characteristics, location requirements, and social relations of industrial sectors not only determine its spatial modes of production, but also the contextual dimension in which the processes of decision-making on M&A transactions take place. Against the background of the differring structural and locational features of the old and the new economy and the various strategic dimensions underlying the recent wave of M&As, corporate takeovers can not merely be seen as the outcomes of atomistic utility maximisers. They rather result from decisions of individual economic actors involved in corporate strategy; these actors are embedded in structures of social relations through which they communicate their decisions and within which power relations shape the choices that are made (Bathelt and Glückler 2002, 2003).

The choice of an M&A target depends on regular communication within and between firms. Thus, the decision-making process on an M&A transaction builds on competencies that are distributed among a variety of different economic actors. This requires collective action and interactive problem solving. Corporate mergers consequently constitute social processes and relational phenomena, taking place in the particular context of a specific location or industry (compare also Dicken and Malmberg 2001; Bathelt and Boggs 2003).

Along with being contextual, M&As are also relational in that they are path-dependent and contingent: M&A activities are based on past, often irreversible actions that determine future corporate strategic decisions. In that way, a firm's target choice (or its attitude towards a takeover bid) relies on its experienced values resulting from previous transactions. That is, the trajectories of the involved firms affect their characteristic actions in a merger or acquisition; yet the way in which M&As shape future corporate strategy and interactions thereby remains rather uncertain or -predictable.

This relational perspective has distinct consequences for understanding M&A decisions, the role of context-specific attributes in corporate takeovers, and the consequential spatial outcomes of corporate mergers. At first, contextuality implies that changes in the structure of M&A activity are resulting from strategic decisions which are path-dependent and contingent. The path-dependency and contingency of M&A decisions, in turn, causes different takeover patterns. Being bound to a particular set of locally embedded agents and institutions, moreover, M&A decisions are context dependent and vary therefore significantly across different locations and particularly industries. As the adjustment of dynamic conventions and relations requires the co-presence of agents and is most efficiently conducted through co-location (Storper 1997), geographic proximity and agglomeration economies are particularly relevant when studying M&A activity.

3.2 The reshaping of economic activity in Germany by means of M&As

Given the theoretical reflections on the strategic determinants and the role of contextual attributes in M&A activity, its spatial implications, and the conceptualisation of corporate takeovers as relational processes in the previous sections, the following hypotheses are derived:

> ➤ The wave of M&As in Germany in the last decade has led to a profound restructuring and relocation of economic decision-making and activity which is considerably influenced by economies of proximity and agglomeration. The most distinct consequence of these trends is an increasing concentration of firms in large urban areas and an emerging archipelago economy.

> This change is characterised by significant time differences and dynamics. While economies of proximity and agglomeration become growingly important, the role of geographical distance in M&A activity is a waning one. A panorama of 'rising metropoli' predominates which is characterised by an exalted and increasing degree of metropolitan interconnectivity (see chapter 2).

> As outcomes of contextual and path-dependent strategic corporate decisions, the patterns of M&As vary significantly across different industries, most notably between the new economy and more traditional, mature manufacturing industries.

Following a brief description of the data base and a concise exploration of the applied analytical instruments and operationalisations, the remainder of this section focuses on the first two of these hypothesis and explores the changing economic geography in Germany as a consequence of the recent wave of M&As and its spatial dynamics in general. The industry specific differences of M&A activities in the 1990s are subsequently addressed in section 3.3.

3.2.1 Data and methodology

As the most comprehensive record available for recent M&A activity in Germany, the M&A Review database provides information on more than 29,000 events that took place in the 1990s with a German firm involved and classifies, if possible, each acquisition by location, industry and type.[18] As with all data sources on M&A (see e.g. Green and Mayer 1997; Chapman and Edmond 2000), unfortunately, there is little information on the value of the transactions, i.e. a takeovers' economic significance; nevertheless, the frequency counts clearly indicate the overall level of M&A activity and its wide-ranging trends.

Methodologically, three analytical modules are applied: The first step encompasses the estimation of a location quotient that – standardized by regional GDP – designates the relative quantity of M&As in each of the 40 German Regierungsbezirke, the administrative unit below the Länder. In order to picture the general pattern of M&A ac-

---

[18] The database is maintained by the University of St. Gallen and can be accessed via the platform GENIOS Wirtschaftsdatenbanken (http://www.genios.de). Due to missing entries as well as methodological reasons (see below) the present study do not cover all of the total of 29,385 transactions, of which 7,765 are transnational (compare also chapter 2).

tivity in Germany, the index is visualized in a series of maps which highlights the most substantial changes within the German geography of M&As during the period of investigation. Having excluded the cases for which no exact geographical information is given, this step of the analysis covers an overall of close to 24,600 corporate takeovers contained in the database in which the acquiring firm was a German one.

The analysis then turns to the different markets of M&As across the various German sectors and focuses at first on a total of 19,034 intranational transactions, excluding the cases for which the dataset provides no industry-specific information. The aim of the second analytical module is to set up a basic classification of the specific characteristics between different sectors in terms of the spatial dimensions of their takeover activities. For this purpose, the analysis includes the following ten industries, which allow for a comprehensive illustration of how M&A specificities vary across sectors: financial services, insurance, and transport industries, as well as media and ICT for the new economy; and heavy manufacturing, automotive, and energy, as well as the chemicals, and textiles, on the other side. In these ten industries – representing, with regard to M&A activity, the most dynamic in Germany (M&A 2003) – more than 11,000 intranational deals were conducted in the 1990s.[19]

The second analytical module executes a descriptive examination of the M&A specifics across the ten selected industries, in which the two determinants that form the basis for the provided classification framework are operationalised as follows: Economies of proximity are measured by the number of M&As that have been conducted within the same Regierungsbezirk, i.e. when the acquiring firm and the target are both placed in the same, relatively small territory. Metropolitan interconnectivity indicating the archipelago economies in Germany is estimated by the proportion of transactions undertaken only within and between the six most important German M&A metropoli, i.e. Frankfurt, Dusseldorf, Hamburg, Munich, Berlin and Cologne (see chapter 2).

The final step of analysis is a multiple regression analysis that, in essence, constitutes the estimation of a gravity model.[20] In logarithmic form, the model which has

---

[19] In total, the M&A Review database comprehends 18 sectors. In excess of the industries included in the analysis presented here, these are the building and construction sector, general services, electronics and medical technology, retail, aerospace, precision engineering, nourishments and luxury articles, as well as the paper industry.

[20] In human geography, gravity models evaluate or forecast the various kinds of flows of goods, people etc. between origins and destinations (spatial interaction). In basic Newtonian form, they are expressed as follows:

$$I_{ij} = k M_i M_j Dist_{ij}^{-\beta}$$

been individually regressed on the record of M&As in each of the ten marked industries adopts the following form:

$$MA_{ij,t} = \alpha + \beta_1 \ln GDP_{i,t} + \beta_2 \ln GDP_{j,t} - \beta_3 \ln Dist_{ij} + \varepsilon$$

wherein the number of M&As that took place between region i (in which the acquiring firm is situated) and region j (locating the M&A target) in each year of investigation t (1990-99) is a function of the regional *GDP* in the two involved Bezirke, indicating the respective level of agglomeration, as well as the geographical distance between the acquiring firm and its target.[21] The estimates of the economic effects, i.e. the correlation coefficients, are depicted by β_1, β_2 and β_3 respectively; finally, α denotes the constant and ε the error term. As the regressions are conducted for every year in the database, a dynamic picture of the concentration processes at work in each of the investigated sectors as well as the changing role of geographical distance in the geography of M&As emerges.

3.2.2 An emerging archipelago economy?

Overall, the German economic geography of M&As in the 1990s is marked by three important characteristics. First of all, corporate takeovers in Germany are economic processes in which economies of proximity and agglomeration play a foremost role. By far the greatest share of M&As occurs either within the same Regierungsbezirk, or as a transaction in which the acquiring firm is located in a large metropolitan area: On average, in more than a third of all intranational M&As, the acquiring firm as well as its target have been located in the same Bezirk. Apart from localisation economies (external to the firm, internal to the industry) and urbanisation economies (external to the industry, internal to the local economy), i.e. benefits form skilled labour pooling, knowledge spillovers and scale economies in infrastructure provision, for instance, also institutional investors deserve special attention in this regard. For financial intermediaries such as the Länder, banks and insurance companies – which

---

where I_{ij} denotes the interaction between two locations i an j; M_i and M_j represent the 'masses' measuring the strength of i and j (usually the population numbers of two settlements), $Dist_{ij}$ stands for the distance between i and j; and k and β are constants (compare e.g. Robinson 1998).

[21] The data for GDP_i and GDP_j are compiled from the German Statistisches Bundesamt for each year during the period of analysis t (1990-99). The variable distance is linearly approximated via the spatial gravity centroids of the two regions concerned.

play a particular role in the 'German model' of corporate governance as the primary owners of companies on the local and regional level (Gorton and Schmidt 1996; Streeck 1997; Berndt 1998; Franks and Meyer 2001; Wójcik 2002, Clark and Wójcik 2003) – distance would be a significant obstacle in exercising control. Further major reasons for the overall relevance of intraregional M&A deals relate to local embeddedness (Granovetter 1985; see also Glückler 2001; Hess 2004), the aforementioned locational assets and localised capabilities and, not least, the possibility for frequent personal or 'handshake' interaction, face-to-face communication, and 'emotional closeness' (Leamer and Storper 2001; Storper and Venables 2004).

The significance of agglomeration economies for M&As in Germany is even more striking if only the most important German M&A metropoli are taken into consideration. Their intraregional transactions alone (i.e. not the M&As performed between, but only within them) account for almost a fifth of all intranational Germany M&A events. This figure rises to 22.3%, if the top ten German agglomerations are regarded (in addition to the six key nodes already mentioned, these are Stuttgart, Karlsruhe, Hanover and Bremen). Overall, more than 55% of all intranational transactions have been performed from the six most important M&A metropoli only; and if again the top ten German M&A urban regions are taken into account, almost 70% of the overall German acquiring activity is concentrated in large metropolitan areas.

In favour of Veltz' archipelago economy hypothesis, the second characteristic of the German M&A economy signifies the interconnectivity of the important M&A metropoli. With increasing shares, the events that took place only within and between the six largest German metropolitan areas amounted to close to 33% of all intranational transactions. If only the M&As conducted from the six key nodes are considered, the intercity transactions account for even more than 60%. This can be taken not only as a strong indication for the argument that economic decision-making becomes increasingly concentrated in a small number of agglomerations; in addition, this implies a growing scope of intercity connections and a progressively strengthening of the interactions and linkages between these points of control at the expense of their regional contexts.

The third important aspect determining the spatial distribution of M&As in Germany, finally, relates to the factor distance: Once the factor agglomeration is taken into consideration, corporate transactions take place between nearby cities, rather than at larger distances. This fact corresponds to the findings of Wójcik (2003) who also demonstrates that geography must be regarded a crucial dimension in the German model of corporate governance:

"[P]roximity breeds corporate ownership and control links, and corporate governance, even at the subnational level, is by no means spatially uniform" (Wójcik 2003: 1455).

Accordingly, companies tend to be controlled by entities that reside nearby – a result that holds true even though the great deal of diversity in the German model of corporate control depending on company age, size, sector and further characteristics. With regard to the most recent trends and dynamics of 'Deutschland AG', however, the relevance of distance, as well as the trends towards centralisation and increased urban interconnectivity, did not exhibit stable patterns during the last decade, but varied in a significant manner.

3.2.3 The territorial dynamics of M&As in Germany

At the beginning of the last decade, the first years after the reunification, the overall German geography of M&As is characterised by marked differences between the spatial distribution of acquiring firms and M&A targets (see Fig.3.1). As the two maps illustrate, the restructuring and the reorganisation of production in the former GDR triggered a significant number of intranational M&As between Westerns and Eastern firms, with Western firms mainly as the acquirers.

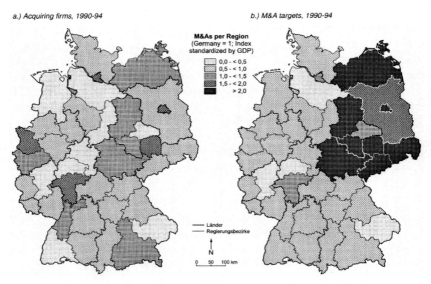

Fig. 3.1. Acquiring firms and M&A targets in Germany 1990-94

On the target side (Fig. 3.1b), all Bezirke in the New Länder display above average M&A activities in relative terms, i.e. after standardisation by regional GDP. Leipzig (showing a *MApR-I* location quotient of 3.60), Dresden (3,05) and Chemnitz (2.64) (the three Saxonian regions), Magdeburg (3.44) and Halle (3.05) in Saxony-Anhalt as well as Thuringia (3.09) and Mecklenburg-Western Pomerania (2.88) present the regions from which the greatest number of firms has been acquired. Acquiring firms, on the other hand, were principally located in the large Western metropolitan areas, among them first and foremost the most important German M&A metropoli Frankfurt (Regierungsbezirk Darmstadt, 1.71), Dusseldorf (1.70) and Hamburg[22] (1.70). Furthermore, the capital Berlin (1.79) became a primary preferential location for corporate headquarters in the German M&A economy (compare also Krätke 2001). Above average levels of acquirers are also to be found in Mecklenburg-Western Pomerania (1.10), Magdeburg (1.24), Halle (1.28), and Leipzig (1.52); due to the high number of targets in these regions, in balance, they nevertheless experienced a significant loss of corporate control. This loss of control in Eastern Germany can be stated as the overall characteristic of the German M&A economy in the early 1990s.

Turning to the second half of the 1990, remarkable changes occurred in this pattern of a distinct East-West direction of corporate control, where the only exception was marked by the increasing relevance of Berlin as headquarter location. Now, the M&A panorama is at first a rather balanced respectively aligned one in which regions with a high quantity of acquiring firms locate an above average number of targets, too (Fig. 3.2). Yet again, notwithstanding the standardisation by regional GDP, the most striking feature of this panorama is the primary dominance of large urban areas. Beside Hamburg (2.02), Dusseldorf (1.80) and Frankfurt (1.73) as, again, the three most important acquirer locations, only the regions situating one of the three remaining key M&A metropoli Munich, Cologne, Berlin, as well as Bremen, Stuttgart (both representing Landeshauptstädte, i.e. the capital cities of the Länder) and Rhinehesse-Palatinate exhibit an above average of acquiring firms.

Now, when focus is shifted to the target side again, a rather similar picture emerges. Compared to the first period, the distribution of targets is much less dispersed. The two city states of Hamburg (1.84) and Bremen (1.76), as well as in Halle (1.79) in Eastern Germany exhibit the greatest relative concentration of targets. But also Frankfurt (1.41), Dusseldorf (1.34), Berlin, the Munich area (both 1.24) and Co-

---

[22] Note that the location quotients for the three city states Berlin, Bremen, and Hamburg might be slightly overestimated, as within their administrative borders no hinterlands exist.

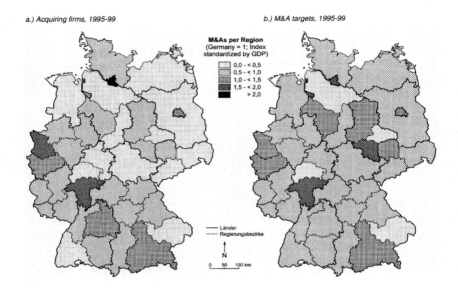

Fig. 3.2. Acquiring firms and M&A targets in Germany 1995-99

logne (1.13) represent regions from which an above average quantity of firms was acquired. That is, in the second period, the six identified principal M&A nodes embodied not only the most dominant locations of acquiring headquarters, but also accounted for the largest proportion of M&A targets.

In close connection to this structural change, the degree of metropolitan interconnectivity experienced pronounced alterations over the last decade, too. Whereas in the early 1990s the share of Frankfurt, Dusseldorf, Berlin, Hamburg, Munich and Cologne merely accounted for close to 30% or less of all German intranational M&As, since 1995 this proportion continuously lies above 34%. If the inter-city transactions between the six identified M&A metropoli are related to the sum of events conducted exclusively from these locations, the same holds true, namely an increase from the range between 52.7% (1991) and 59.4% (1992) in the first years of the period of investigation, to constantly more than 62% in the mid 1990s and a maximum of 64.9% in 1999.

The panorama of an increasing overall relevance and interconnection of agglomerations in the German M&A economy likewise becomes obvious, when it is turned to the results of the regression analysis. Displaying the correlation coefficients resulting from the year by year estimation of the above specified model on the whole dataset23, Fig. 3.3 reveals the dynamics in the statistical association between the number of M&As between two regions and the independent variables geographical distance and economic agglomeration.

At first, the depicted regression results demonstrate that the early 1990s experienced a particularly pronounced concentration of economic activity, where M&As tend to happen with the acquiring firm generally located in a larger agglomeration than the target. This finding is in accordance with the analysis of the location quotients, in which the variances between the regions situating most notably acquiring firms and those where targets dominate have been substantially greater in the early 1990s than in the second period of investigation.

The second half of the 1990s, in contrast, is characterised by a profound shift towards M&As taking place above all among large metropolitan areas, as most notably revealed by the rise in importance of size and agglomeration economies of the target's locality (GDP_j) and the decreasing gap between both locations involved in a transaction.

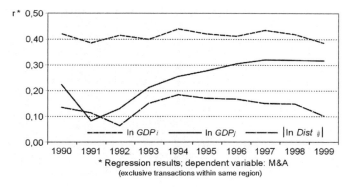

Fig. 3.3. *The changing relevance of agglomeration economies and geographical distance in the German M&A economy*

---

[23] Needless to say that the cases in which the acquiring firm and the target are located in the same Regierungsbezirk were excluded from the analysis. An inclusion of these events would cause a profound overestimation of the variable distance.

Fig. 3.3 also denotes, finally, the extent to which the role of geographical distance in the German M&A economy changed over time. Right after the reunification, when Western firms first of all tended to acquire targets in the former GDR, this determinant appeared to play a rather small role. Yet subsequent to the first few years of profound restructuring in East Germany and the early 1990s recession, distance emerged as a likewise important factor for the spatial distribution of M&As, which – though progressively losing relevance, in particular if compared to the increasing role of the degree of agglomeration of a target's locality – never turned statistically insignificant during the period of investigation. Taking this insight on the changing role of distance together with the findings reported afore, the overall economic geography of M&As in Germany can be regarded as the product of essentially two, overlaying dimensions: Whereas in the early 1990s, the general restructuring of industrial production in consequence of the reunification was characterised by processes of intense economic concentration, in the late 1990s, a pattern dominated that can be labelled as an scenery of 'rising metropoli' (compare also chapter 2).

3.3 Industry specifics in German takeover activity

Across different industrial sectors, however, distinct deviations emerge from this strongly aggregated picture. Discussing the various markets for corporate takeovers in more detail, the following therefore accounts for the specific M&A-related differences across industries and the interdependencies between industrial structures and location attributes in the German M&A economy.

3.3.1 Classifying the markets of M&As

With reference to the results of the descriptive examinations of the data set, Fig. 3.4 provides a basic framework that classifies the investigated sectors according to their M&A specific characteristics. The resulting industry clusters are determined by the role that geographical proximity plays in the patterns consequential to M&A decisions and the degree of metropolitan interconnectivity in an industry's takeover performance.

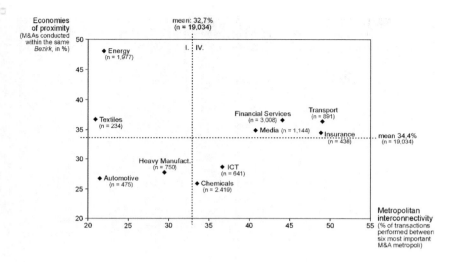

Fig. 3.4. M&A specificities across German industry sectors: Economies of proximity vs. metropolitan interconnectivity

Industrial sectors are thus allocated to four quadrants. Media, financial services, transport and insurance are all in the first quadrant, showing above average relevance of both geographical proximity and metropolitan interconnectivity. In all four industries, the share of takeovers performed within the same region is close to 35%, while more than 40% of transactions take place within or between the six German most important metropoli. The second quadrant comprises the chemical and IC/TC sectors. M&As in these sectors are featured by above average metropolitan interconnectivity, but spatial proximity plays a smaller part than in the four industries in Quadrant I. The heavy manufacturing and automotive sectors can be found in Quadrant III, indicating below average importance of proximity and metropolitan interconnectivity. M&As would thus have contributed to a greater relative dispersal of these activities, with respect to the concentration experienced in the majority of the other sectors. Finally, M&As in the textile and energy sectors have – with the automotive sector – the lowest proportion of intermetropolitan takeovers, but are heavily determined by proximity (951 of 1977 M&As in the energy sector in the 1990s took place within the same Regierungsbezirk).

The differences in the role of economies of proximity and intermetropolitan connectivity detected among the ten sectors are reinforced by the diversity of the results of the gravity regression model for each sector reported in Figure 3.5 (for more details, compare also Appendix 1).

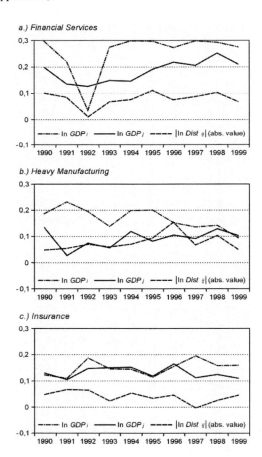

Fig. 3.5. M&A specificities across industry sectors: Results of the yearly regressions

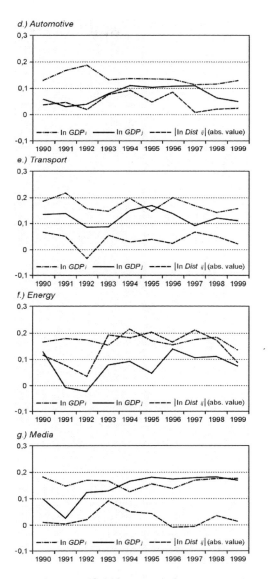

Fig. 3.5. M&A specificities across industry sectors (cont.)

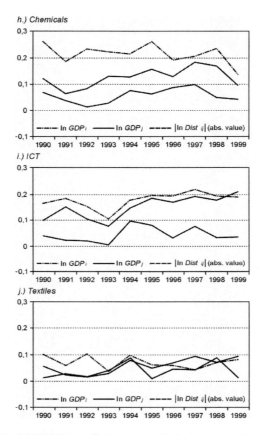

Fig. 3.5. M&A specificities across industry sectors (cont.)

Here, the importances of the role of the size of the markets of the acquiring and the acquired firm and of distance vary significantly from one sector to another. When the criteria reported in Fig. 3.4 (economies of proximity and metropolitan interconnectivity) and the variables included in the regression analysis (tendency towards concentration and relevance of distance) are combined for each sector, an extremely variegated picture emerges (Tab. 3.1).

Tab. 3.1. The German markets of M&A: Classification of industries

Industry sector	Economies of proximity		Metropolitan interconnectivity		Tendency towards concentration		Relevance of distance	
	total relevance	dominant trend	total relevance	dominant trend	total relevance	dominant trend	total relevance	dominant trend
New economy								
Finance and transport								
Financial Services	+	→	++	→	+	→	+	→
Insurance	+	↓	++	↓	+	↑	=	→
Transport	+	→	++	↓	+	→	-	→
Creative industries								
Media	+	↑	+	↑	=	↓	insignificant	
IC/CT	=	↓	+	↑	=	↓	insignificant	
Old economy								
Traditional 'heavy'								
Heavy Manuf.	=	→	=	→	+	↓	+	→
Automotive	=	→	-	→	+	→	=	↓
Energy	++	→	-	↓	+	→	++	↑
Traditional 'light'								
Chemicals	=	→	=	→	+	→	=	→
Textiles	+	↓	-	→	-	↓	insignificant	

Legend: ++ particular important   = low importance   ↑ increasing relevance   → stable relevance
         + important   - mostly irrelevant   ↓ decreasing relevance

This picture is one in which a straightforward division between the factors that drive M&As in more traditional and knowledge-intensive sectors – or, oversimplifying, between an 'old' and a 'new' economy – is nowhere to be seen. Economies of proximity are important in some traditional industries, such as textiles and energy, but also in the knowledge-intensive financial service and insurance sectors, as well as the creative media industry. In ICT among the knowledge-intensive sectors, and automotive and heavy manufacturing among the more traditional ones, their role is, in contrast, almost negligible. Similarly, there is a strong tendency towards concentration in large urban areas in some of the knowledge-intensive sectors like finance and insurance again, just as in several traditional industries (e.g. heavy manufacturing or energy). Distance, finally, is relevant for sectors as dissimilar as financial services and energy. Hence, more than a traditional vs. knowledge-intensive or 'old' vs. 'new' division of the geography of M&As in Germany a fourfold division seems to emerge.

3.3.2 New economy

Finance and Transport: The concentration of economic activity in metropolitan areas as a consequence of the wave of M&As in the 1990s is most noticeable in the German financial sector as well as the insurance and the transport industries. In almost every third out of four transactions in the transport sector, for example, the acquiring firm was headquartered in one of the identified six metropoli; and in the two finance service industries, this share amounts is only little less than 70%. As revealed by the highest levels of inter-city M&As among all examined industries (Fig. 3.4), firms in the finance and transport business benefit primarily from inter-metropolitan relations; proximity, i.e. to aim for a target being located in the same region than the acquirer, is yet a second major feature of the takeover activity in these industries. The recent merger of Dresdner Bank in Frankfurt and the assurance company Allianz AG, Munich, or the Bavarian HypoVereinsbank, emerged from Bayerische Hypotheken- und Wechselbank and Bayerische Vereinsbank (both located in Munich) in 1998, may serve as examples illustrating the particular role played by economies of agglomeration and localisation in this category.[24]

This pattern reflects the archetypical behaviour of the so-called 'progressive' services firms which depend first of all on accessibility and proximity to each other. These firms benefit from good physical access to customers, a vast range of other local business activities, and from large pools of qualified labour and educational achievements in urban areas. Readily accessible transport facilities, a competitive market environment as well as availability of high-quality telecommunications infrastructure and quality office accommodation are further location attributes of predominant relevance in these industries. Once it is taken into account that M&As have led to a greater geographical concentration in agglomerations, also distance appears as an significant factor relevant for the takeover activity. Principally in financial services – with more than

---

[24] In some of the cases above regulation has also played a key role in determining M&As. German capital markets are heavily regulated at the Länder level, making geography a crucial dimension in the German model of corporate governance (Wójcik 2002).

3,000 transactions in terms of M&As by far the most dynamic German sector in the 1990s – there is thus a greater chance that firms acquire a target in neighbouring rather than in far away urban areas.

Media and ICT: In contrast to what might be expected, the wave of M&As in the media[25] and ICT industries does not seem to have led to a considerably greater concentration of activity. This is related to the fact that the great majority of the companies in these sectors tends to be small and do not benefit from significant economies of scale. Furthermore, these are the real sectors in the new economy: highly mobile, increasingly relying on telecommunications networks, and, in general, less dependent on R&D activity than sectors like automotive or chemical. In fact, distance appears as an insignificant factor for corporate takeovers; that is to say that M&A transactions at greater distances, such as the acquisition of a call centre in a rather peripheral region for instance (Graef 1998), are more likely to occur than in finance, energy, or heavy manufacturing. For the time being, this result points to Quah's notion of a weightless economy which emphasises the radical possibilities of the cost-free reproduction and distributions of e-goods such as software or multimedia services, and in which firms depend rather on high-quality communication facilities than close personal contacts, i.e. on traded rather than untraded interdependencies, to use Storper's language again.

On the other hand, however, takeovers in media and ICT were also considerably affected by proximity and inter-metropolitan links – although to a slightly lesser extent than finance and transport. In both industries, the relevance of interurban connections is above average, and close to a third of all events still took place in the same region. These characteristics, in contrast, now once more point to the significance of social interaction, the importance of a creative environment, or handshake transactions and face-to-face communication. In sum, both traded and untraded interdependencies represent therefore significant factors shaping M&A activity in media and ICT.

3.3.3 Old economy

Traditional 'heavy' industries: M&A activity in heavy manufacturing, automotives and energy is driven foremost by economies of scale. The completion of the liberalisa

---

[25] Concerning the German media industry, it is noteworthy that, beside Hamburg, Cologne and Munich, several important industry clusters exist also in rather small cities, like for instance Leipzig or Potsdam-Babelsberg (compare e.g. Bathelt and Boggs 2003; Krätke 2002, 2003).

tion of the German energy market in 1998 provoked extensive changes in the German energy sector (e.g. Haas and Scharrer 1999) and the bulk of the more than 900 local, rather small energy distributors was acquired by one of the then eight German Verbundsunternehmen (transmission system operators), i.e. the companies active in the high-voltage dispatch sector, like EnBW, the RWE Group or EON.Net, the latter being created from the merger of PreussenElektra-Netz and Bayernwerk Netz. Potential benefits from size and consolidation have furthermore led to profound restructuring in automotives (e.g. Hudson and Schamp, 1995; Schamp 2000), and even more distinctively in heavy manufacturing. Though in this sector, the share of transactions conducted from the six identified German centres of corporate control amounted to considerable 53% (compared to 42% and 38% in automotives and energy respectively), overall, urbanisation and economies of agglomeration affect all three industries to a rather smaller extent in comparison to other sectors.

Likewise, geographical distance and economies of proximity appear as minor players in automotive and heavy manufacturing. In energy, however, proximity and distance relate most expressively to corporate takeovers, with companies either merging in the same region, or acquiring others in nearby, rather than in distant areas. This picture has to be seen against the background of the need for large plants in these mature industries (in which headquarters tend to locate close to their plants), and most notably the costs of space in large urban agglomerations. Moreover, the level of R&D conducted in these industries is relatively small; proximity and association to research centres and universities located in metropolitan areas is thus only to a lesser extent relevant. In sum, the dominance of economies of scale can be seen as the major driving force behind the wave of corporate consolidation in these sectors. In particular with regard to energy and heavy manufacturing, location specifics have nonetheless proved to represent further significant factors that also in mature manufacturing industries remarkably determine the spatial outcomes of corporate takeovers.

Textiles and Chemicals: The German textile industry underwent profound restructuring processes and most notably a significant decline already before the reunification (Hassink 2003; Haas and Zademach 2005). In consequence, this sector shows by far the lowest number of M&As and has to be regarded the least representative in the sample. Nevertheless, its contextual characteristics are rather similar to the heavy manufacturing and automotive, with the predominant factor being economies of proximity, whereas the industry was barely driven by agglomeration economies and distance, and much less prone to concentration. This reflects that R&D activities are once more relatively unimportant and points to the extent to which textile plants are likewise sensitive to the rising cost of space in large urban areas.

The German chemical sector, finally, exhibited yet again an extensive reshuffling in the 1990s (Bathelt 1997). Though this industry was most notably affected by the changing global environment and transnational mergers were consequentially rather frequent (compare e.g. the case studies by Bathelt and Griebel 2001 or Zeller 2000), distinct concentration process emerged on the national arena as well. Metropolitan interconnections, distance, and proximity, on the other hand, appear as minor factors in corporate takeovers in this industry. The overall M&A pattern of the chemical sector thus replicates an industry which simultaneously operates in both narrow local clusters and complex relations between subcontractors, service providers, and integrated corporate units across the entire nation as well as the globe.

3.4 Conclusions

Corporate takeovers and mergers constitute an expression of the information-based and globalised socio-economic formation of the late 20th and early 21st century that reflect the ongoing restructuring of production processes in an increasingly competitive environment in particularly expressive manner. Though M&As, especially when regarded in their totality, have consequently significant implications on the local, regional and global scale, they yet remain a rather rare object for investigation on the geographical research agenda. Taking the German economy as an illustrative case, this chapter has illustrated the dynamics and the extent to which the most recent wave of corporate consolidation led to a profound relocation of economic activity and an increasing concentration of corporate power and control in large urban areas.

Furthermore, the analysis has highlighted the diverse combinations of factors at play across different industries. The various markets of M&As are affected by similar forces of economies of proximity, concentration and agglomeration, although in significantly different ways from one sector to another. Physical distance is another important factor, as there is relatively little sign – with the exceptions of the media industry, as well as information and communication technologies – of geography losing importance in economic transactions. Even in some knowledge-intensive sectors, such as finance and insurance, proximity plays as important a part as ever, casting doubts on the much-publicised existence of general trends towards the emergence of a weightless economy or the end of geography. From this perspective, M&As represent both a symptom and a cause for the increasing concentration of economic decision-making in large urban areas and of the rise of of the economic power of large metropolitan areas.

To account for the various location specifics of different industries is a task of particular importance for future explorations of corporate takeovers and their spatial logics. Further comparative examinations and case studies that take into consideration both the sector-specific spatial implications of M&As and the varying roles of location factors across industries will be suggestive for this purpose and may contribute to a comprehensive economic geographic conceptualisation of corporate takeovers and mergers.

4 THE CHANGING ECONOMIC GEOGRAPHY OF EUROPE: EVIDENCE FORM M&A ACTIVITIES[26]

A substantial and at least until most recent times extensively rising proportion of the pronounced wave of mergers and acquisitions (M&As) that featured most of the developed economies since the mid 1980s (UN 2000) has been cross-border. During the 1900s, the number of corporate takeovers taking place between companies of different national origin or home countries grew more than six-fold (Kang and Johansson 2000, compare also chapter 2) and accounts today for more than every third transaction. A significant share of these activities has been focused on Europe, where it was stimulated by the process of economic integration (e.g. Brenton et al. 1999, OECD 2000). Concerning this matter, Fig. 4.1 displays some recent trends for both the number of transactions and their respective deal values upon the basis of the Mergermarket database, a comprehensive dataset covering more than 15,000 M&A events with involvement of an European firm.

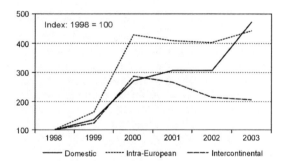

Fig. 4.1a. Trends in M&A activities involving European firms (1998-2003, by number of events)

---

[26] The author would like to thank Sasha Cole, Natalie Galluccio, Hans-Dieter Haas, Peter Maskell and Andrés Rodríguez-Pose for their comments on earlier drafts of this chapter. He is highly grateful to all experts interviewed for the time and efforts they devoted to the project as well as Vassilis Monastiriotis for the guidance with the econometric model. Generous financial support of the German Research Foundation DFG (grant HA 795/8-1) and provision of research facilities at the Department of Industrial Economics and Strategy of Copenhagen Business School in September 2004 and are also thankfully acknowledged. The usual disclaimers apply.

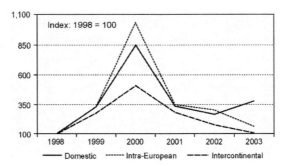

Fig. 4.1b. Trends in M&A activities involving European firms (1998-2003, by deal volume)

The graphs depict all transactions covered in the database from the outset of recording in 1998 to 2003 inclusively, an important period of changes and challenges in Europe, comprising the implementation of the European Monetary Union (EMU) and immediately before the Eastern enlargement in 2004. Calibrated with reference to an index, they distinguish between 'domestic' transactions, in which the firms engaged are located in the same country, 'intra-European' events involving companies from at least two European nations, and 'intercontinental' deals where European firms are either acquiring non European ones or represent the target of a European-non European transaction. As regards the sheer number of transactions (Fig. 4.1a.), the figure first reveals that, notwithstanding global markets for firms and announcements of spectacular 'deals' becoming less exuberant in the early 21st century, the overall level of M&As involving European firms and the induced pace of corporate and industry restructuring (Clark 1989; Dicken and Öberg 1996) remain remarkable.

Second, the graphs highlight that the tendency towards increased cross-border interaction – with the number of international, i.e. overseas and intra-European transactions rising more rapidly than domestic ones – lasted for the most part only until the year 2000, the historic heyday of international M&A euphoria (Fig. 4.1b.). From 2001 onwards the trend of internalisation became sharply reversed and domestic markets appear to gain relevance again. This distinct reversal indicates the impacts of the downturn of the global economy, the stock market collapse, or the happenings of September 11th 2001 (Jansen 2002). As Tab. 4.1 exhibits, this process is paralleled not only by decreasing overall volumes, but also by sharply declining mean deal values.

Tab. 4.1. Aggregate volumes and mean deal values of domestic, intra-European and and intercontinental M&As involving firms based in Europe[1], 1998-2003

Year of observation	Σ deal volumes (in billion Euro)					
	1998	1999	2000	2001	2002	2003
Intercontinental	111,2	304,4	561,2	311,1	195,9	118,1
Intra-European	55,4	183,4	569,8	194,3	166,2	89,9
Domestic	90,8	301,4	767,6	302,5	239,4	343,9
Total	257,4	789,2	1898,6	807,9	601,5	551,9
	Mean deal values (in million Euro)					
	1998	1999	2000	2001	2002	2003
Intercontinental	320,5	707,8	567,5	338,9	265,0	166,3
Intra-European	252,0	512,2	606,8	216,6	188,6	92,5
Domestic	204,4	500,7	639,7	222,9	177,4	163,9
Overall average	254,6	567,7	607,0	254,7	202,5	145,0

Note: [1] including all 43 countries of contemporary Europe in its encyclopaedic geographical scope

The central purpose of the chapter is to present new empirical insights on transnational corporate mergers as "recent developments of enormous economic geographical impact" (Markusen 2001) and to explore the "inadequately understood implications" (Chapman and Edmond 2000: 754) of these financial transformations with regard to European production system as a whole (see also Chapman 2003). In this manner, it unfolds the shifts and displacements of corporate control consequential to the M&A activities between 1998 and 2003 involving firms located in the (former) European Union of 15 members, the ten new member states and the four EFTA countries Switzerland, Norway, Liechtenstein and Iceland at the aggregate level.

As corporate takeovers, by definition, decisively affect the nature and the boundaries of the involved companies, the chapter additionally aims to provide a contribution to the (discipline-specific) conceptualisation of the firm. Interlinking the still rather small amount of literature addressing M&As from the specific spatial point of view (e.g. Green 1990; Ascroft and Love 1993; Anand 1995) with the seminal work focusing on the concept of the firm and its requirements in economic geography (see e.g. Dicken and Malmberg 2001; Taylor and Asheim 2001; Maskell 2001; or Taylor 2004), an approach is proposed which attempts to incorporate a contextual, location-specific perspective into existing perceptions of firms and their performance, competitiveness and evolution. Particular attention is thereby paid on economies of proximity and agglomeration and local sources facilitating the production of knowledge as determinants of the firm and corporate takeovers, as well as on the interconnection between M&As and the process of regional integration in Europe (section 4.1).

Based on this approach and subsequent to some methodological reflections relevant for the conducted analysis (section 4.2), the chapter first examines the scope to which the wave of M&As at the end of the last decade and the beginning of the new millennium contributed to alter the shape of the location of economic activity and decision-making in Europe (section 4.3). By combining quantitative, macro-perspective insights with qualitative empirical findings on the firm- or micro-level[27], it then addresses the factors that may explain the detected levels and patterns and indicates the extent to which M&As ought to be regarded not merely as purely strategic, organisation-specific and 'footloose' activities, but also as 'spatially determined', i.e. location-driven or contextual economic actions (section 4.4). The concluding section evaluates the proposed explorations, discusses their limitations and offers directions for future research.

4.1 On firms, M&As and economic integration

Primarily through leverage on growth and employment, firms have significant effects on space and places (compare e.g. already Storper and Walker 1989). In this context, M&As represent an effective tool to execute this locational impact, though this impact comes into view not always by means of direct physical establishments like greenfield investments, but, for instance, through the relocation of decision-making functions or shifted power relations in the governance of a regional economy. The general effect of M&As tends to be re-organisation of industrial assets and production structures on the global scale (Kang and Johansson 2000: 34), which can lead to greater overall efficiency, without necessarily greater production capacity (OECD 1996). Furthermore, cross-border M&As facilitate the international movement of capi-

---

[27] The present chapter exhibits some results of a fundamental component in a larger research project on the spatial determination and implications of M&A supported by the German Research Foundation (DFG). Up to submitting this draft in October 2004, only a fraction of the qualitative investigations planned for the 16 month overall project horizon has been conducted. The citations and quotes given here are consequentially to be regarded rather anecdotal evidence. A list of all hitherto interviewed firms and institutions (including the positions of the conversational partners) as well as the interview guideline are reported in Appendices 2 and 3.

tal, technology, goods and services and the integration of affiliates into global networks. With regard to the host economy, cross-border takeovers or mergers may be effective in terms of capital accumulation, employment effects, technology transfer, increased competition and efficiency gains (compare also the corresponding effects of FDI, on which a survey is given e.g. in Werneck 1998). Foremost, however, corporate takeovers or mergers, shifting decision-making functions from the acquired object to the bidder company, lead to a pronounced displacement of economic power of which the clearest consequence is a cumulative, self-energising concentration of executive authority in already existing control nodes (Green 1990; Clark 1993; Chapman and Edmond 2002; compare also chapter 2).

As already indicated, the main focus of this chapter in hand is to expose an investigation of the impact of M&As on the spatial organisation of corporate control in Europe, i.e. the territorial *implications* of corporate takeovers. In order to cope with the topic of investigation in its all-embracing spatial relationality, the chapter yet also tackles the inverse direction of the causal association between firms and M&As on the one hand and local or regional economic systems on the other, thus the *determination* of M&A transactions by location-specific, contextual factors. In other words, the question is addressed if the spatial perspective, or the 'geographical lens' as Bathelt and Glückler (2003) put it, provides insightful information on the reasons why firms engage in mergers or acquisitions and whether firms are thus determined by space and place. In particular, the chapter strives to understand how firms engaging in M&As evaluate the role of spatial proximity and 'localised capabilities' (Maskell and Malmberg 1999), i.e. essentially external scope economies that local firms may enjoy from co-location and their access to (innovative) suppliers, customers and competitors as well as further local knowledge sources like universities and a skilled labour pool.

Here, one camp has been arguing that firms and industries are becoming more and more footloose and economic activities progressively take place regardless of physical distance. In fact, cross-border M&As are considered not merely as symptom, but a central reason regarding this matter, where geography is treated more or less as historical relict (as discussed in more detail in the two previous chapters). There exists, however, a counter-movement that follows a radically different line of thinking. According to this view, spatial proximity enhances the competitiveness of firms by facilitating the types of interrelations and interactions that keep organisations in place and foster processes of learning and innovation by means of face-to-face contacts and 'local buzz' (Storper and Venables 2004). In this line of reasoning, proximity acts as a basic governance mechanism in that it reduces transaction costs by establishing helpful local codes and a common language (compare Maskell et al. 2004).[28] Similarly, Morgan (2004) warned against accepting views regarding the supposed death of geography, as knowledge creation still depend on localised interaction to a large extent. Thus, a specific geographical configuration of economic activity is seen as playing a crucial role in determining the future prospects of firms.

Against this background it appears essential to address the firm in microtheoretical terms, although the quantitative executions remain foremost on the aggregate, i.e. macro level. Within the economic geographic literature on corporate takeovers in macro-perspective, endogenous theoretical accounts specifying the role of location factors as determinants of firms extending their boundaries by means of M&As are far apart, if at all existing[29]; instead, the studies on M&As conducted in the discipline usually borrow theoretical notions developed in neighbouring fields, such as e.g. Dunning's (1977, 1979) eclectic paradigm (see also chapter 2) or Porter's (1990) diamond.

The approach presented in this chapter pursues the opposite direction of reasoning; instead of applying external concepts to a geographical piece of research, it aims to enrich business and managerial perceptions of firms and M&As by core economic geographical insights. Incorporating the role of contextual factors into the competence-based view of the firm[30] – which, built on the seminal work of Penrose (1959), apprehends firms as heterogeneous assemblies of assets under a common direction leading to a stream of valuable products or services – a simple, specific geographical configuration of the firm is suggested. This approach enables, it is argued, the analyse of both firms engaging in M&As and the economic systems where the involved firms are located.

---

[28] Of course, proximity between actors located in different parts of the world exists, thanks to modern technological and institutional developments that make easier both the transfer of information and the travelling of people, also in relational sense. This is however beyond the scope of this chapter.

[29] This observation also applies to the bulk of studies conducted in managerial sciences and business economics; compare e.g. Dunning (1998): "Location and the Multinational Enterprise: A Neglected Factor?"

[30] The competence-based view fulfils the empirical and theoretical economic geographical requirement to be applicable on different levels of spatial aggregation (Maskell 2001; Zademach 2002). Also for this reason it is appropriate for the present piece of research which addresses predominantly the level of nation-state.

4.1.1 Conceptualising the firm in economic geographical terms

In most recent years, the theory (or concept) of the firm received a considerable amount of attention in the discipline. A crucial factor initiating the discussion was the observation that the firm has frequently been mentioned in the writings of economic geographers, but it traditionally remained a vague entity without a clearly defined form or function:

> "In most of economic geography literature, there are few structured discussions, hardly any definitions, and almost no reflections on what actually constitutes a firm, what roles it performs in the economy and why it exists." (Maskell 2001: p. 329)

The approach suggested here conceptualises firms as entities which are best captured by means of combining three perceptions, namely first an organisational (or institutional), second an interaction-orientated, and third a contextual or spatial perspective on the firm (Fig. 4.2).[31] It thus combines and complements insights from rather established theories of the firm, like e.g. the *neo-classical, institutionalist, behavioural* and *structuralist* perspectives, or the *embedded network, discursive-performative* or *temporary, connected coalition* interpretations (see for an overview on the theories of the firm e.g. Foss 1999; for specific economic geographical perceptions, compare Martin 2000; Yeung 2000, 2001b, 2002; Dicken and Malmberg 2001; Taylor and Asheim 2001; Taylor 2004).

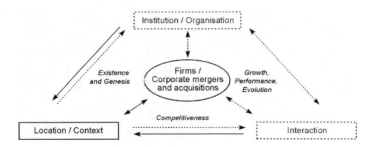

Fig. 4.2. Conceptual framework to analyse the implications and determination of firms and M&As

---

[31] Note that the suggested framework is to a certain extent adjacent to Schamp's (2003) reflections on "space, interactions, and institutions" as three basic perspectives in (German) economic geography.

Regarding the organisational, institution-specific viewpoint, the proposed approach conceives the firms as units of production, determined first by the intention to generate profits and create personal wealth by means of producing goods or services (cf. Taylor 2004), and second by specific ownership structures (e.g. Grossman and Hart 1986). According to Niman (2004: 275), the firm provides a framework that creates economically meaningful relationships by constraining and supporting the interaction between individual competencies; as institutional structures, firms assume importance by giving unique competencies an economic role to play in the creation of value.[32] The institutional building block thus addresses a company itself as a formal institution and repository of competencies which is predetermined by its corporate strategy, -governance, -culture, -history and -identity, and most notably its competencies. Consequently, this perspective allows controlling for microtheoretical, organisational concerns by accounting for a firm's unique competencies and the coordinating mechanism that brings them together.

The extensive amount of literature on pre- and post merger integration management or processes exhibits that firms as well as M&As are rather well studied topics in this regard (for a more detailed review of the literature addressing M&As from a corporate and strategic point of view, compare chapter 3 again). However, this managerial literature on M&As either remains widely detached from a firm's locality, its environmental interlinkages, agglomeration economies etc.[33], or disregards the significance of these aspects. Concerning this matter, Lorenzen and Mahnke (2002: 4) note in their study on the acquisition of local knowledge in regional clusters that "the MNC literature downplays the role of mergers or acquisitions as an entry mode."

Within the second constituent, the proposed approach permits to enlarge this introversive view on the firm by the role of formal institutions exterior to them. It perceives firms as interacting with other organisations, foremost subcontractors, competitors and clients, but also regional economic associations or non-governmental organisations, thus being embedded in functional, socially constructed networks of reciprocity and interdependence (Grabher 1993; Stroper 1997). Hence, the approach incorporates inter-organisational interaction, cooperation and communication (compare e.g. Foss 2001), processes of interactive learning (e.g. Bathelt and Boggs 2003) or repeated ac-

---

[32] Following Maskell et al. (1998) the expression 'competencies' is used when referring to firms, 'capabilities' is applied when referring to territorial entities only.

[33] Exceptions do, indeed, exist, especially as regards the comparison of different entry modes (i.e. joint ventures vs. greenfield investments vs. M&As) into regional clusters (e.g. Kuemmerle 1999; Frost 2001).

tions in regional or global value chains, production networks and projects (e.g. Gereffi and Korzeniewicz 1994; Henderson et al. 2002; Grabher 2002) as determinants which shape a firm's genesis, evolution and performance – and, in turn, their locations – just as well as the set of factors internal to the firm.[34]

Accounting for the reciprocal relation between firms and their surroundings, the conception finally incorporates within the third, contextual constituent that organisations do not only impact on their environment, but are also significantly influenced by their locations and territorial context. As already Chandler (1977) has pointed out, changes in the environment (e.g. the development of mass transportation systems) led to substantial alterations in the structure of firms. In view of that, contextual factors external to an organisation, i.e. a location's endowments, image or identity, including localised knowledge and resources, effects of spatial proximity, institutional settings, legal frameworks, economies of agglomeration and urbanisation, transport costs, governance and power relations as well as conventions, norms, traditions etc. (or untraded interdependencies, to use the words of Storper 1997) at the regional, national or supranational scale, represent a set of factors that configures firms and their boundaries not merely in a subordinated manner, but in a comparable way as the first two sets of determinants. More specifically, the context-specific building block regards firms as a repository of competencies which are, when bidding for an M&A target, to a great extent determined by the challenge to internalise localised capabilities (exposed in more detail in the next subsection).

The three perspectives addressing firms and their behaviours, boundaries, and external relations when engaging in M&As are profoundly interconnected and intertwined. By means of accounting for their interplay, the suggested approach is appropriate for a rather embracing analysis of the implications of firms and M&As on regional systems on the one hand, and the impact of regional endowments or localised capabilities on a firm's performance and M&A motivations on the other. In a single article it is however not possible to take into consideration all aspects in full detail that under other conditions would merit closer scrutiny. Hence, the present chapter primarily pays attention to the location-specific constituent (against the background of its in-

---

[34] The determination of firms as embedded networks and the associations between M&As and agent-network-relationships (as well as their interdependencies with location- and organisation-specific factors) are not at the core of this chapter. Future research on the firm level may provide valide insights on the extent to which institutional re-arrangements or organisational restructuring consequential to M&As alter network relations on the different geographical scales.

terconnection with the remaining two) and addresses the role of contextual factors in general and localised knowledge capabilities in particular as determinants of firms and M&As in more detail now, followed by the interconnections between M&As and the process of economic integration.

4.1.2 Contextual influences as determinants of firms and M&As

M&As are prompted by a range of factors including excess capacity or increased competition, but foremost by new market opportunities and the need to acquire complementary firm-specific intangible assets, such as human resources, brand names, technologies etc. (Kang and Johansson 2000: 3). Essentially through agglomeration economies, i.e. positive externalities that benefit local firms, these intangible assets are considerably influenced by a firm's locality (Saxanien 1994; Porter 1998). According to the competence theories, firms can be furnished with valuable heterogeneity by using specific factors in their surroundings that are not equally available to competitors elsewhere (Maskell 2001: 338n). Firms without any major internal competencies or valuable resources are able to survive and thrive if they are favourably located, just as the competitiveness of otherwise identical firms may diverge as a consequence of the way in which difference in location shows up in their strategy. A firm's location and country of origin therefore directly affects its choice of strategy (Collis 1991).

Initially, the heterogeneity between localities may have been caused by variations in the natural resource endowment. Today, however, it is seldom the inherited natural properties, but rather the 'created localised capabilities' – including "the specific, but basically random first-mover advantage in some particular skill or technology, differentiated patterns of demand and supply, disparate results of past investments, distinctive formal and informal institutional endowments, and dissimilar technological assets, all of which may make territorial entities differ from one another" (Maskell 2001: 339) – that enable firms to exchange otherwise purely internal information and establish the platform of heterogeneity on which the competitiveness of firms can be built and augmented. If a firm does not possess sufficient intangible assets to be competitive, it may seek them in the asset bundle of an existing local firm through acquisition (Kang and Johansson 2000: 32). Then again, as a firm accumulates more and more intangible assets, it has stronger incentives to exploit them, e.g. through geographical diversification and access to new markets.

The gravity of the market (in terms of both its sheer size and nearby located clients and competitors) on the one hand, and attractive forces of innovative human resources on the other, was repeatedly confirmed in the conducted interviews. Correspondingly, a representative of a Bavarian business development agency responded after questioning for the three most important objectives for foreign firms to acquire local companies:

> "Market. Market and partners – that is to say market potential. We indeed campaign with the fact that Germany, or better the German-speaking region, is the most important market in Europe in terms purchasing power. This is a very important factor. Then, there certainly is also the qualification of the people living here. ... It definitely makes a difference that high technology is located just here. Thus, market and partners, I would say, are the most important issues." (Interview 26.08.2004)

Within the contextual perspective, the present approach explicitly incorporates the here mentioned factors as determinants of a firm's competitiveness and its incentives to increasingly accumulate intangible assets by means of internalisation and geographical diversification. Though not all embracing, but to a reasonable extent, these assets can be accounted for through controlling for the quality of the labour pool, e.g. in terms of capacities for innovations (absolute number of patents) or its share of investments in R&D. The level of education and patents per capita (as an estimate for the efficiency or output of the educational system) exemplify further appropriate variables displaying localised capabilities.

Studies that are more regional in their geographic scope (e.g. Ò hUhallachàin 1994 or Anand 1995 on M&As in the US and the Canada respectively) or address a certain industrial sector (e.g. Lagendijk 1995; Shan and Song 1997; Chapman and Edmond 2000; Lorenzen and Mahnke 2002; Nuhn 2004) reveal additional factors relevant for M&A activities and patterns. According to the North American experiences of Green (1990: 133), market size as well as similarity in language, legal structure and geographical proximity can explain the dominance of the UK and Canada in the US market. Analogous trends have been detected in the German market of M&As, where the neighbour states likewise account for the dominant fraction of cross-border takeover activities (Zademach 2004).

As cross-border engagement induces transport costs for both goods and human capital and effective corporate governance typically becomes more difficult and costly the more distanced – geographically, functionally and culturally[35] – the owner is from the economic activity, physical distance between the home and the host market

---

[35] On the different dimensions of distance, compare e.g. Lo (2003: 122n).

remains essential (Morosini 2001, Sekkat and Galgau 2001, Uppenberg and Riess 2004; Bertrand et al. 2004). In the same way, a target location's overall investment climate or country risk determines firms and their M&A behaviours. Finally, the context perspective also subsumes the impact of modifications in the institutional setting on the supranational level. Particular attention is therefore pinpointed now to the interrelation and interdependencies between firms and M&As and the process of European integration.

4.1.3 Cross-border investments in the light of regional integration

In the EU, the number of M&As increased by more than two and a half times between 1987 and 1998. Apart from being related to the evolution of the economic cycle (Rodríguez-Pose 2002: 24), most analysts agree that cross-border investments in general and M&As in particular appear strongly stimulated by the process of economic integration.[36] Substantial evidence is therefore given first by the sharp increases of both intra-European as well as intercontinental transactions targeting the European market in the late 1980s and in the early 1990s, i.e. in anticipation of the completion of the Single European Market (SEM). After the completion of the SEM, the number of intra-European deals declined and stagnated at approximately three times the level of the mid 1980s (e.g. Kang and Johansson 2000).

Further evidence for the impact of economic integration on corporate takeovers is the major surge in European M&A activity in the preparation of the EMU in the second half of the 1990s prompting the Financial Times to describe 1998 as the 'year to end all years' with reference to M&As (Chapman and Edmond 2000). With regard to the latter part of the decade, OECD (2000: 13) states that "the deeper market integration in Europe with the introduction of the Euro has facilitated cross-border operations in the participating countries". Consistent to these *a priori* expectations concerning the effects of economic integration (compare also chapter 2), the Eastern enlargement appears similarly anticipated – "Business is always far ahead politics" (cf. Interviews 12.08., 11.09. and 12.09.2004) – and expectantly longed for by the actors in the European M&A markets.

---

[36] Clegg (1996) as well as Srinivasan and Mody (1997), however, display a rather ambiguous picture.

The spiralling of M&A activities in Europe was yet not only propelled by the completion of the Single Market and the expected economies of scale linked to the launch of the Euro; above all, it has to be seen as self-energising, cumulative process. The new global economic actors resulting from mergers of large transnational companies increasingly drove other companies to look for partners or acquisitions. Furthermore, this trend was related to supportive financial conditions, i.e. high stock prices that encouraged companies to expand through mergers (as target companies could be acquired in exchange for generously valued shares of the acquiring company), and changes in the policy environment. Regulatory reform and privatisation, most notably in telecommunications and the energy sector, played important roles in the global merger boom, making cross-border company unions possible where regulations and state ownership had earlier barred such developments. There consequentially is a certain risk of overestimation and exaggerated euphoria when it comes to the impact of economic integration on cross-border investments. Turning to the analysis of the most recent developments in European M&A activities now, it is therefore crucial to keep in mind that the ultimate economic justification of corporate mergers is to increase profitability and competitiveness (as addressed in the suggested threefold approach by the firm-interior, institutional perspective), with financial conditions, policy adjustments and institutional changes serving less as key driving forces, but rather as catalysts.

4.2 Methodological foundations and specification of analysis

Comprising firms and M&As in the proposed, threefold manner allows light to be shed on how its association with regional integration and other explanatory variables can be assessed. More specifically, the following set of hypothetical derivations is stated on the basis of the outlined literature review and theoretical considerations.

> - Apart from organisational and strategic aspects on the micro-firm level (institution- and agent-network/interaction-related determinants), the trend of increasing concentration of firms, administrative power and corporate control in the existing control nodes of Europe, i.e. the strongest European economies, is assumed being likewise influenced by context dependant factors, most notably localised capabilities and economies of agglomeration and proximity.
> - The considerable positive effects of geographical neighbourship detected in the studies displaying a more regional scope, i.e. that cross-border transactions

emerge particularly frequent between direct neighbour regions and countries, are in this connexion presumed to occur across the whole of Europe.

➤ In accordance with the outlined observations on the effects of the completion of the SEM, the extent to which the target's location is involved in the different stages of the process of European integration is expected to present a further influencing variable for the patterns and levels of M&As. However, this effect should not be overestimated as the market anticipates and internalises the advancements in the integration process earlier than they in fact come into play.

Before focus is shifted to the examination of these hypothetical derivations, the subsequent paragraphs give a brief description of the database and reflect on the methods applied.

4.2.1 Data description and preparation

Recording every European M&A transaction with a transaction volume exceeding Euro 5 million since 1998 (North American content from 2003 onwards), the Mergermarket database represents a uniquely extensive, if not comprehensive coverage of recent takeover activities in Europe. For each reported event[37], the information contained includes the dates of announcement and completion, the identities of the acquiring and the target company, their respective locations (i.e. country), and the value of the transaction (in million Euro and/or GBP and US$) together with the source of this information. Furthermore, a brief deal description sheds light on the nature of the stakes held by the acquirer (e.g. Management Buy Out, 80% of assets etc.). This textual information proved helpful with regard to the – on first sight indeed rather 'thin' – locational record, revealing that in the case of 1,189 transactions the stakes of one of the involved companies were shared across varied economies.[38] In spatial terms, such events represent not only one transaction, but multiple. Assuming that the control over the target

---

[37] Originally, the dataset covered an overall of 18,633 completed transactions between 1998 and 2003. Including the 1,763 entries constructed by means of the 'splitting' procedure, the augmented dataset encompasses close to 20,400 M&A events, of which the ones without European involvement were excluded from the present analysis (see also Appendix 4).

[38] This is the case, if the bidder, for instance, is either a transnational joint venture (like e.g. EADS, the European Aeronautic Defence and Space Company, of which the stakeholders are Dutch, French, German and Spanish), or a company which's majoritarian assets have already beforehand been acquired by a foreign corporation.

firm is 'split' between the acquirers (and thus between the countries locating them) pursuant to their respective holdings, each of these cases has been multiplied in correspondence with the number of involved economies; the deal values were proportionately subdivided.

Despite the fact that the dataset, prepared in the described manner, can be regarded a powerful and promising tool for research on corporate takeover activity, it shares some of the limitations with which other sources of information on M&As are afflicted. A considerable shortcoming is the fact, that more than every fifth entry lacks the deal value (Tab. 4.2), i.e. precisely the record making this database so unique and valuable.[39] Though this proportion is doubtless a harmful loss, it leaves us, on the

Tab. 4.2. Description of Mergermarket database as prepared for the analysis

Year of observation	1998	1999	Number of M&A events 2000	2001	2002	2003	Total	
Overall dataset	**1,011**	**1,390**	**3,128**	**3,172**	**2,970**	**3,781**	**15,452**	
European firms[1]							events	(%)
as bidder	848	1,206	2,757	2,781	2,580	3,366	**13,538**	848
as target	827	1,144	2,510	2,645	2,621	3,486	**13,233**	827
Transatlantic	347	430	989	918	739	710	**4,133**	347
Intra-European	664	960	2,139	2,254	2,231	3,071	**11,319**	664
Domestic	444	602	1,200	1,357	1,350	2,099	**7,052**	444
Cross-border	220	358	939	897	881	971	**4,267**	220
Deal value missing	63	101	580	715	785	1,340	**3,584**	63
Focus of analysis[2]			Number of M&A events					
	1998	1999	2000	2001	2002	2003	Total	
EU 15								
as bidder	810	1,154	2,562	2,552	2,341	2,980	**12,399**	810
as target	785	1,056	2,242	2,328	2,255	2,952	**11,618**	785
EFTA								
as bidder	29	44	157	149	147	192	**718**	29
as target	24	45	135	133	127	202	**666**	24
New members								
As bidder	2	6	21	42	37	61	**169**	2
As target	8	29	72	108	145	153	**515**	8

Notes: [1] including all 43 countries of contemporary Europe in its encyclopaedic geographical scope
[2] Σ bidders = 13,286; Σ targets = 12,799

---

[39] Compare Chapman and Edmond (2000: 757): "One of the most fundamental drawbacks of this [i.e. the one used in their study on corporate restructuring in the EU chemical industry] and other sources of M&A information is that simple counts [number of events] describe the level of economic activity, but not necessary its economic significance."

other hand, with almost 80% and a total of 11,868 transactions where this information is given.[40] In the conducted investigations, this problem is encountered by means of considering both, i.e. the deal values and the number of events, in all steps of the analysis.

4.2.2 Formalisation of the spatial determination of M&As

In order to examine the impact of M&A activities on the economic geography of Europe on basis of the just described data, the investigation comprises three steps. The first of them analyses the relative frequency of transactions in the 29 selected European economies. That is, in accordance with the methodology applied when investigating the German market of corporate mergers and takeovers in the second chapter, the main nodes in the European takeover economy are first identified through the estimation of a location quotient. Via standardisation by national GDP, the index $MApC_{(gdp)}$-I controls for the overall level of economic activity in each economy and masters the extent to which a country is indeed affected by M&As.[41]

The value added of this method, compared to the division of the number of bidders through the number of targets[42] as presented e.g. in Green and Meyer (1997) and

---

[40] In the original dataset, i.e. before preparing it in terms of its all-embracing spatial coverage, this proportion amounted to close to 21% and thus remains almost unchanged by the splitting procedure.

[41] $MApC_{(gdp)}$-I is calculated according to the following formula:

$$MApC_{(gdp)} - I = \frac{\sum_{t0}^{t1} MA_i \,/\, \sum_{t0}^{t1} GDP_i}{\sum_{t0}^{t1} MA_{Eur29} \,/\, \sum_{t0}^{t1} GDP_{Eur29}}$$

MA thereby depicts the absolute number respectively volume of M&A transactions and GDP the national gross domestic product; t_0 and t_1 denote the period of analysis, i stands for the included countries as the regional unit of analysis; $Eur29$, finally, corresponds to the whole of the selected nations, i.e. the sum of their respective annual GDPs between 1998 and 2003.

[42] Note that such ratios are even so given in Appendix 5. It is interesting to note as well that, with regard to the sheer number of events, Greece and Belgium are detected as net gainers in the present study, contrasting the results of the two mentioned, previous investigations. Further slight changes occur in Denmark (turning to a net loser) and Italy (featuring here a rather even balance, beforehand a negative one). Yet overall, the picture of losers and gainers in the trade in corporate control identified by means of these specific ratios appears to present itself as a rather stable one.

Chapman and Edmond (2000), is the relative reflection of M&A activity which encounters the fact that the economic performance of small countries, like e.g. Ireland or Denmark, is often remarkable:

> "Their macro-economic tools are efficient: for instance, if they decide a fiscal policy aimed to attract foreign direct investors, the relative impact of such strategies is higher than in bigger countries, where the effect must be shared with a much broader domestic capital." (Veltz 2004: 10)

The second step explicitly examines the cross-border balances of the considered countries. Finally, multiple regression analysis addresses the factors that may explain the detected levels and patterns of takeover activities and thus, to a certain extent, also the determination of the involved firms. Here, the number of M&As and their aggregated deal values are regressed on the series of variables identified in the theoretical and literature reviewing section in Poisson and Ordinary Least Square (OLS) regressions respectively; while OLS format is adequate for the transaction volumes as continous variable, the Poisson satisfies the count nature of merger data when addressed in sheer number of events (Anand 1995).

Against the background of the methodological limitations of this way of proceeding – foremost, it faces the problem that many of the variables hypothesised to impact on the territorial distribution of M&As (e.g. GDP, agglomeration economies, patent activity or investments in R&D) are likely to be affected by M&As themselves[43] – the results of the econometric exercises are complemented with insights from the qualitative examinations. This means allows encountering the critique that gravity models typically lead to rather robust results in large number observations (e.g. Robinson 1998), too.

---

[43] Further restrictions are: (1) the kind of M&A (conglomerate, horizontal, efficiency- or strategic-asset seeking etc.; (2) the variations among the factors related to specific countries and industries; (3) the means of measuring the effects of the EMU and the Eastern enlargement, i.e. to construct a quantifiable proxy for something that is only very difficult to quantify, like the removal of non-tariff barriers in the case of the eastern enlargement, for instance); and (4) the assumptions made on the counterfactual (or 'alternative position'), thus what is assumed to would have happened in the absence of the EMU and the imminent enlargement (for more details see e.g. Dunning 1997). To some extent, these restriction are however resolved by dint of controlling for spatial autocorrelation and multicollinearity.

4. The changing Economic Geography of Europe

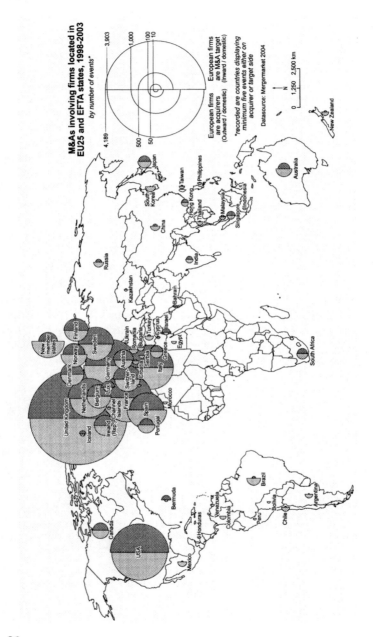

Fig. 4.3. The European market of corporate takeovers at global scales: M&As involving firms located in EU25 and EFTA states, 1998-2003 (by number of events)

4.3 The changing Economic Geography of Europe – Insights from the descriptive examinations

A combination of quantitative and qualitative insights may indeed be considered as leading to the most and clearest pieces that might be found fitting into the puzzle portraying the effects of an integrated Europe on economic activities in general and M&As in particular. The following description of the detected levels and patterns of corporate takeovers across Europe might serve as a primary piece of this puzzle.

4.3.1 Preliminary observations

According to the Mergermarket data, European firms were engaged in 15,452 M&A events exceeding the Euro 5 million threshold during the period of investigation. With 85.9% and 82.8% on the acquiring and the target side respectively, the bulk of this activity is covered by the member states of today EU25 as well as the four EFTA countries. More than 13,200 firms have been acquired from a company located in one of these 29 countries, and close to 12,800 times a firm situated in this selection of economies presented the target of an M&A transaction. Comparatively, the remaining countries of Europe in its geographical sense – Belarus, Ukraine or Romania, for instance – represent rather minor agents, particularly as hosts of acquiring companies (see also Tab. 4.2, again).

As illustrated in Fig. 4.3 and Fig. 4.4, depicting all transactions with involvement of firms located in the EU and EFTA member states at global scales, by far the greatest part of these activities is restricted to the European continent itself. Depending on measurement – i.e. number of events vs. deal values and inflow vs. outflow M&As – this share amounts to near to every third (Fig. 4.4) and 82% (Fig 4.3) as regards the outflows, and 85% and 86% respectively at the inflows. In view of that, the conducted research pays most attention to intra-European transactions.

The general overview provided in Fig 4.5 and 4.6, representing the results of the exercise to calculate the location quotient *MApC-I* for the number of events and the aggregated deal values[44], offers an indication of the overall involvement of the Euro-

---

[44] The exact individual values of the indices are displayed in Appendix 6.

4. The changing Economic Geography of Europe

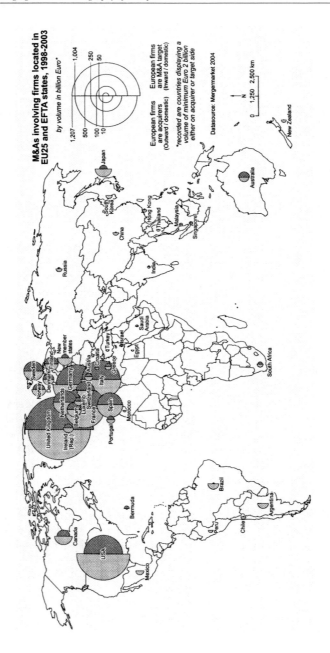

Fig. 4.4. The European market of corporate takeovers at global scales: M&As involving firms located in EU25 and EFTA states, 1998-2003 (by volume of transactions)

88

pean economies into the international trade of corporate control and decision-making functions. Primarily, this step of the analysis shows that in both ways of measuring pronounced, albeit complex differences become obvious regarding the extent to which the European economies are affected by overall M&A activities.[45] Whereas the established members of former EU15 thereby exhibit at first sight a fairly balanced degree of involvement in M&As, characterised by more or less similar values on both acquiring and target side, the new members come into view rather exclusively as targets.

The highest overall acquiring activities are found in the UK, the Netherlands and Luxemburg as internationally well established headquarter locations. Though Greece, Cyprus or also Italy exhibit below average values, other peripheral countries, like the Republic of Ireland, the Scandinavian economies, Spain or even Iceland (at least when M&A activity is measured in sheer numbers) display relatively high $MApC-I$ values on both the acquiring and the target side. France, Germany, Belgium and Austria in the European core, on the other hand, appear being in relative terms much lesser affected by M&As. It thus can be stated as second finding that accounting for a country's overall level of economic activity shows that relatively small, often peripheral economies are similarly or even more heavily affected by M&A activities than agreed strongholds in takeover business in the European core (i.e. the UK, Germany and France, cf. UN 2000).

Thirdly, the two figures pinpoint to the existence of certain dispersal effects which an economy radiates on its neighbouring country. In particular if accounted for the number of transactions, but also when considering the deal volumes, in the majority of the cases, two neighbouring economies are to be found in two adjoining categories, or even within the same category (like, among others, Portugal, Spain and the Scandinavian countries in Fig. 4.5b, or France, Spain and Italy in Fig. 4.6a). The great exceptions to this rule are made up by the UK, Luxemburg, the Netherlands and Switzerland as location of acquiring firms due to their already afore-mentioned outstanding role in the European M&A economy.

---

[45] Systematic distortions due to the cases where the volume/deal value record is missing have been controlled for. An evidentiary general bias could not be detected. Austria, however, where close to half of all entries lack the respective deal volume, has to be regarded a critical case.

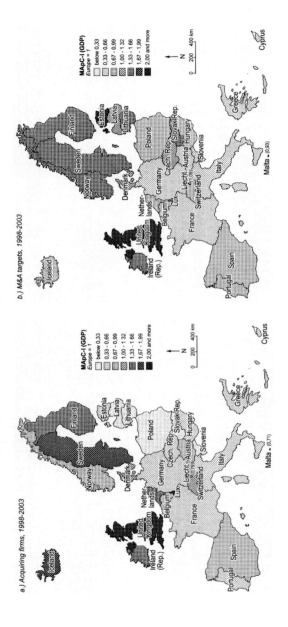

Fig. 4.5. Territorial distribution of acquiring firms and M&A targets in Europe, 1998-2003 (by number of events)

Finally, the *MApC-I* exercise reveals that there occur noteworthy differences between the simple counts and the respective transactions volumes in the detected levels and patterns of M&As. Primarily, this is the case in the new member states, where the volumes are markedly lower than the numbers of transactions at first sight suggested. Though, in principal, the same features the remaining peripheral economies, i.e. Greece and Cyprus, Norway, Ireland and Iceland, as well as Portugal on the target side, this trend is much less pronounced here. In fact, only Germany, Italy and France display higher values in terms of transaction volumes than in terms in sheer numbers. Luxemburg and Liechtenstein add to these three economies, if not both sides are regarded, but only the targets.

Taking both considerations together, the one of the number of transactions and the one of the respective deal volumes, the findings of this step of the analysis demonstrate that – except for the new member states, where external control is clearly increasing – the usual core-periphery division does not hold for the M&A case. Instead, the relative tall number of rather small transactions characterising most of the European periphery points to pronounced industry restructuring processes in these economies. That is, firms located in economically 'stronger' peripheral countries – like the Scandinavians, the Republic of Ireland, and Iceland, all of them performing well above the European average as acquirers – obviously deploy M&As as a powerful tool to increase their competitiveness by means of (intra-national) industry consolidation and to access the European core.

4.3.2 Cross-border M&A activities

As supplement and in order to deepen the just pictured portray of the European M&A economy with regard to the most gaining and losing economies in the trade of corporate control, Fig. 4.7 exhibits the cross-border balance for each considered country by number on the ordinate and value on the abscissa (see also Appendix 5). Turning back to a market's absolute relevance, the figure first highlights, in accordance with the analysis of the location quotients, the outstanding role of the UK (indicated by the aggregated deal values displayed through the overall size of the respective 'bubbles'), followed by Germany and France.

Whereas France belongs, similar to the UK, the Netherlands, Switzerland, Finland, Greece and Island, to the economies in which corporate control becomes increasingly

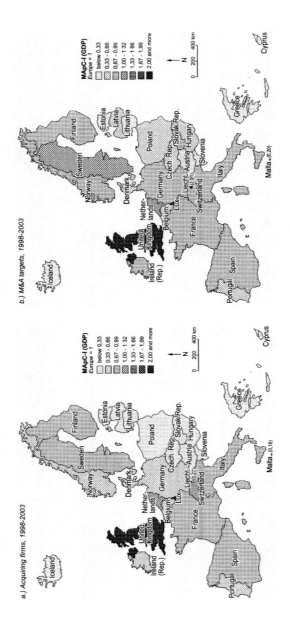

Fig. 4.6. Territorial distribution of acquiring firms and M&A targets in Europe, 1998-2003 (by volume of transactions)

concentrated (as the respective cross-border balances show a positive sign), Germany emerges as the location from where most companies are acquired from, thus becoming more and more externally controlled.

On the one hand, this implies that the German economy and the firms located here are rather susceptible to become the target of a corporate takeover due to economic struggling or weaknesses in their overall competitiveness. However, the selling-off of Germany-based companies rather relates to the fact that this market is among the most central ones in Europe, even gaining in centrality given the Eastern enlargement (Interview 26.08.2004). Moreover, the German economy still possesses a strong pool of skilled labour as well as an above average knowledge and innovation base, i.e. contextual factors making German firms fairly attractive takeover targets.

Further economies losing ground through corporate control being shifted to foreign locations are Norway, Poland and Portugal as well as the majority of the Central and Eastern European countries, foremost Hungary and the Czech Republic. All of them share the characteristic to be located in direct physical neighbourhood to at least one distinctly stronger economy (like Germany in the cases of Poland and the Check Republik, Sweden as regards Norway, or Spain for Portugal) to which long-term economic interactions and dependencies exist in particular due to labour cost advantages.

A third group of countries emerges, where the balance differs depending on means of measurement (albeit having, again, controlled for the missing volume cases). This group encompasses above all Spain, which gains in terms of deal values but loses as regards the sheer number, indicating that the Spanish economy achieves more and more control on greater firms while losing out in small firms. This relationship is established in the reverse way in Italy, the Republic of Ireland, Austria and Luxemburg. Though slightly less pronounced as in the Spanish case, these economies are gaining corporate control in terms of numbers, but losing in terms of volume, i.e. companies located in these states are acquiring foremost smaller firms, while their greater corporations are becoming increasingly externally controlled.

In Belgium, Cyprus, Denmark, Liechtenstein and Malta as the remaining set of countries, the balance appears rather unbiased, indicating either an indeed equalised international exchange of control, or a more or less negligible market size.

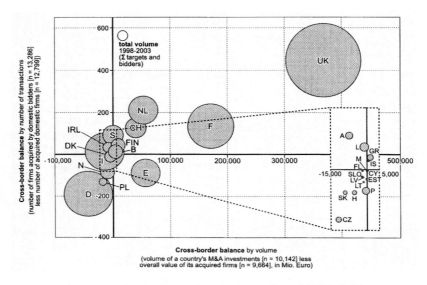

Fig. 4.7. Cross-border interactions in the markets of M&As in Europe

With reference to the insights from the qualitative investigations and against the background of the proposed threefold conceptualisation of the firm, the following, final section aims to shed some light on the factors that may explain the detected levels and patterns in the changing geography of corporate control in Europe.

4.4 The link between M&As and the new face of Europe: Regression results

The regression analysis addresses the following location factors hypothesised to represent key drivers for firms to engage in corporate takeovers:

> ➤ First, indicators related to a target location's overall market potential and prosperity (i.e. its national *GDP* and average income *GDP/cap.*);
> ➤ second, factors accounting for the relevance of geographical and cultural closeness (*Neighbour* for a country's physical neighbouring states; *Distance*, linearly

approximated via the national spatial gravity centroids; and *Language* addressing countries which feature the same official language, like e.g. the UK, the Republic of Ireland and Malta;

➢ third, determinants of a location's structural endowments (*Education* of labour pool and the *Unemployment* rate);

➢ fourth, *Patents per capita* as a factor signifying a target market's localised capabilities; and

➢ fifth, some indicators reflecting a location's institutional setting respectively the extent to which it is integrated into the process of European integration: a nation's investment climate or country risk (*Invclim*); *EU15*, *EFTA* and *NewMembers* displaying if a country belongs to former EU15, EFTA or the ten most recent members in the Eastern enlarged Union alternatively; and finally *EMU* reflecting the Eurozone.

The latter four variables *EU15*, *EFTA*, *NewMembers* and *EMU*, as well as *Neighbour* and *Language* were constructed as dipolar dummies. Eurostat serves as data source for all remaining variables.

When regressed in bivariate manner, virtually all these determinants are considerably associated at the 0.05 or even 0.01 level of significance with both number and volumes of European M&A activities (see Appendix 7).[46] Therefore, a multivariate model it is more meaningful to control for the most significant influencing factors. The simple correlations resulting from the bivariate exercise, however, give a first, rough indication on the model's accuracy. In deciding which independent variables to include into the final equation, the variables were consequently entered one at a time in a systematic and cautious manner. As 'best solution' in terms of explanatory power, the following logarithmic model[47] could finally be established, in which the number of M&As (and the aggregate of their volumes) taking place between country i and each

---

[46] The mere exceptions are *Education* as well as *Unemployment* and *EFTA* as regards deal values. Primarily, the set of tested independent variables was noticeably greater than the one considered in the final model (see Appendix 7). The determinants not included in the multivariate regressions due to multicollinearity or distortional effects are: the growth rate (measured in terms of GDP) of the target market during the period of investigation ΔGDP, this nation's population POP, its share of GDP invested in R&D and its absolute number of Patents.

[47] Natural logarithms used for the deal values as well as some of the independent variables (*GDP, POP, GDP/cap., Pat/cap.* and *Distance*) encounter problems of non-linearity and statistical outliers. In this way, it is also controlled for megamergers exhibiting extreme high volumes, like e.g. the Daimler-Chrysler or Vodafone-Mannesmann deal.

of the remaining selected European economies j – with the acquiring firm being located in region i – during the period of analysis t_1-t_o is a function of the series of the beforehand identified determinants:

$$\ln M\&A_{i,t1\text{-}t0} = \alpha + \beta_1 \ln GDP_{j,to} + \beta_2 \ln Distance_{i,j} + \beta_3 Neighbour_{i,j} + \beta_4 \ln GDP/cap_{j,to} + \beta_5 \ln Pat/cap._{j,to} + \beta_6 Unemploy_{j,to} + \beta_7 Education_{j,to} + \beta_8 Invclim_{j,to} + \beta_9 Language_{i,j} + \beta_{10} EMU + \beta_{11} NewMembers + \varepsilon$$

Tab. 4.3 and Tab. 4.4 report the outcomes of the estimation of the model in eight steps for the number of events and transaction volumes respectively.

Tab. 4.3. M&A activities in Europe: Estimates of robust Poisson regressions on number of events

Dependent variable: M&A (number of events)	(1)	(2)	(3)	Model (4)	(5)	(6)	(7)	(8)
ln GDP	0.702*** (0.067)	0.676*** (0.063)	0.651*** (0.072)	0.668*** (0.070)	0.685*** (0.069)	0.705*** (0.083)	0.741*** (0.078)	0.698*** (0.088)
ln Distance		-0.928*** (0.098)	-	-0.926*** (0.097)	-0.933*** (0.097)	-0.924*** (0.100)	-0.970*** (0.110)	-0.966*** (0.110)
Neighbour			1.032*** (0.215)	-	-	-	-	-
ln GDP/cap.				0.047 (0.111)	-	-	-	-
ln Pat/cap.					-0.020 (0.058)	-0.047 (0.074)	-0.085 (0.116)	-0.232* (0.123)
Unemployment						-0.013 (0.036)	0.016 (0.037)	0.019 (0.037)
Education						-0.002 (0.006)	-0.0003 (0.011)	0.012 (0.009)
Investment climate							-0.254 (0.194)	-0.293 (0.201)
Language							0.069 (0.255)	0.064 (0.253)
EMU							-0.323 (0.298)	-
NewMembers								-0.551 (0.416)
Observations	812	812	812	812	812	812	812	812
Wald Chi2	110.30	248.18	332.49	248.57	249.57	274.13	352.88	322.07
Significance	<0.001	<0.001	<0.001	<0.001	<0.001	<0.001	<0.001	<0.001
Pseudo R^2	0.296	0.390	0.346	0.390	0.390	0.391	0.402	0.400
Multicollinearity	-	no	no	no	no	no	no	no
Heteroskedasticity	no	no	no	no	no	no	no	no
Spatial autocorrelation	no	no	no	no	no	no	no	no

Notes: unstandardized coefficients reported; standard errors in parenthesis; ***,**, and * denote significance at the 0.01, 0.05 and 0.1-level

Tab. 4.4. M&A activities in Europe: Results of OLS regressions on volumes in logarithmic form

Dependent variable: ln M&A (Σ volumes)	(1)	(2)	(3)	Model (4)	(5)	(6)	(7)	(8)
ln GDP	0.528*** (0.074)	0.553*** (0.070)	0.499*** (0.072)	0.456*** (0.084)	0.473*** (0.083)	0.421*** (0.089)	0.410*** (0.091)	0.376*** (0.102)
ln Distance		-0.995*** (0.180)	-	-0.974*** (0.179)	-0.960*** (0.180)	-0.997*** (0.181)	-0.956*** (0.207)	-0.965*** (0.207)
Neighbour			1.267*** (0.282)	-	-	-	-	-
ln GDP/cap.				0.338** (0.163)	-	-	-	-
ln Pat/cap.					0.136* (0.075)	0.190** (0.086)	0.296* (0.154)	0.194 (0.163)
Unemployment						0.017 (0.034)	0.011 (0.036)	0.016 (0.037)
Education						-0.011 (0.007)	-0.018 (0.013)	-0.009 (0.011)
Investment climate							0.215 (0.231)	0.217 (0.222)
Language							0.135 (0.435)	0.147 (0.434)
EMU							-0.152 (0.389)	-
NewMembers								-0.499 (0.688)
F	51.457	43.524	37.466	30.771	30.337	18.841	11.826	11.888
Significance (F)	<0.001	<0.001	<0.001	<0.001	<0.001	<0.001	<0.001	<0.001
Df	300	299	299	298	298	296	293	293
R^2	0.146	0.225	0.200	0.237	0.234	0.241	0.244	0.245
Adj. R^2	0.144	0.220	0.195	0.229	0.226	0.229	0.223	0.224
Multicollinearity	-	no	no	no	no	no	no	no
Heteroskedasticity	no	no	no	no	no	no	no	no
Spatial autocorrelation	no	no	no	no	no	no	no	no

Notes: unstandardized coefficients reported; standard errors in parenthesis; ***,**, and * denote significance at the 0.01, 0.05 and 0.1-level

In the first three models the overall number of European cross-border M&As is regressed either solely on GDP, or GDP and one of the two measures of geographical proximity (*Distance* in Model 2 and *Neighbour* in Model 3). The displayed results confirm, first of all, the already indicated primary role of the size of the targeted market as the key force to attract foreign investments. Alongside, the findings designate that physical closeness between the acquiring firm and the target – closeness in that as the significant association with *Distance* displays a negative sign – in actual fact emerges as second, powerful explanatory variable for the territorial distribution of M&As in Europe. This corresponds to the already mentioned cases of the US and Germany, confirming the hypothesised, theoretically established role of geographical proximity in the European geography of M&As.

The conducted qualitative work substantiates that this result does not only hold on the national scale but also on the regional and firm level, as the following statement of a Bavarian inward investment advisor might illustrate:

> "If an American or a Japanese firm is coming along, it wants to conquer the European market. They are looking for an option, i.e. where to go to. Particularly Japanese firms increasingly target the German market at the moment. Before, their prime goal was always Great Britain. Now they realize that Great Britain is not [the whole of] Europe ... French or Italian firms, in comparison, do naturally not aim for the European market; they target the German economy as the most well funded market in Europe. In this context, spatial proximity is important for them. Italy and Austria as direct neighbours work fine anyway. France, on the other hand, is yet more difficult for Bavaria; French firms have in mind rather North Rhine-Westphalia, Saarland etc, i.e. the bordering regions. We therefore really have to argue why Bavaria makes sense for French firms." (Interview, 26.08.2004)

Turning back to the regression analysis, the incorporation of the factors controlling for the structural endowment and the institutional setting of a target country led to less satisfactory results. However, this step again exposes significant differences between the sheer number of transactions and the respective deal values. This is the case as regards the average prosperity of the population in a target market, indicated by the variable GDP per capita, where no significant association is to be found for the numbers, but a positive one for the volumes (Model 4). For increasing deal values this implies that M&A engagements become not only more likely between the greatest markets, but that firms – after controlling for their most important intentions, namely entering large new target countries and favouring the closer ones of them – are also in quest of wealthier locations.

The same holds true for the outcome of education as measured in patents per capita: Accounting for the values of the transactions, this factor is robustly associated with the volume of M&As conducted between two countries (Model 5 to 7 in Tab. 4.4). This finding gives certain support for the presumption of firms seeking far and foremost for knowledge related assets when engaging in M&As. The results in Tab. 4.3 appear to contradict this finding; thereby, it yet has to be taken into account that the number of 'small' transactions is rather overestimated when not controlling for the deal value. Together, this indicates that smaller firms (engaging in smaller transactions) are first of all interested in market access to new, preferably close markets, while the internalisation of localised knowledge sources raises with the size of the firm and the transaction volumes respectively (compare also Kuemmerle 1999).

Among to the remaining variables hypothesised by the received theory as meaningful to explain the distribution of cross-border corporate investments, no further significant associations arise when estimated in the multivariate manner. Neither language and investment climate, nor the enlargement variable and whether the economy locating the target is in Euroland or not, emerges as playing a role that is comparable to market size and geographical proximity. To a certain extent, the loosing relevance of linguistic barriers or the levelling country risks point to an indeed deeply advanced process of integration in Europe. And again, analogous to what has already been observed for the merger wave immediately before the completion of the SEM, the M&A business appears to have anticipated – and already implemented – the most recent challenges before they actually came into play.

After all it can be summarised that the territorial distribution of intra-European cross-border M&A activity may be explained by the combination of market power, proximity, and, though to a slightly lesser extent, prosperity and localised sources of knowledge as measured in terms of patents per capita. Institutional factors on the other hand, appear being subordinated to the gravity of the market and the attractiveness of a location's innovative capabilities. In this context, it yet appears essential to account for the deal values and thus the size and structure of the firms involved, as differences between the sheer numbers of transactions are indicative.

4.5 Conclusions

With the purpose to address the determinations and implications of corporate takeover and merger activities in the changing economic geography of Europe, this chapter has explored M&As involving firms located in the EU25 as well as the four EFTA countries between 1998 and 2003. Presenting new empirical findings on an important but somewhat neglected topic, it initially identified the strongest and weakest European economies within the international 'trade' of corporate control and illustrated that small nations, largely located in the periphery, are in part likewise or even more heavily affected by M&As than the established strongholds in this business. Furthermore, the chapter has attempted to provide a contribution to the conceptualisation of the firm

in the discipline. Accounting for the interplay between contextual, institutional (or internal, organisational) and interaction-related factors, the specific economic geographical configuration proposed for this reason perceives firms as bundles of competencies which, when extending their boundaries through engagement in M&A transactions, are distinctly seeking for the internalisation of local sources of knowledge and innovation, also referred to as localised capabilities. Against the background of this concept, it has been demonstrated to what extent the spatial perspective may shed light onto the factors explaining the detected levels and patterns of M&As across Europe.

The results of the combination of qualitative and quantitative empirical methods indicate that access to new and core markets and effects of geographical proximity (to a certain extent also signifying cultural interrelatedness) represent the key drivers in the European M&A economy. Provided that it is controlled for the transaction volumes, local knowledge sources measured in terms of patents per capita emerge as significant determinants of cross-border corporate investments, too. Hence, the internalisation of localised capabilities appears to become more important with increasing transactions volumes, i.e. increasing size of the involved firm. Institutional affiliations, like the deepened process of European integration, assessments of country risk or linguistic barriers, but also structural factors (e.g. unemployment), in contrast, turn out being less influential at the intra-European scale, thus long-term anticipated and internalised by the market.

Due to the missing counterfactual, the analysis of the concrete impact of process of European integration remains a particularly difficult, challenging task which is to be addressed more profoundly in future research. Concerning this matter, the use of an aggregated dummy for the EMU or the Eastern enlargement certainly failed to capture the industry-, firm- and context-specific effects of the respective steps in the process of European integration over time. In consequence, a multiplicity of opportunities for disaggregation comes into view; the here detected patterns may thereby facilitate selections processes. To apply a more differentiated operationalisation of the notion of localised capabilities and to attend closer scrutiny to the interaction perspective are further important tasks in such disaggregate studies. In doing so, the proposed threefold perception of the firm should receive additional conceptual efforts in order to fully transform it from the present synopsis of existing approaches into a discrete and coherent theoretical framework.

Overall, the study has deepened the understanding of firms and corporate takeovers and mergers in that the implications and determinations of M&As which have been identified on the intra-national or regional level were shown being more sophisticated on the supranational level. Though the dominant role the market forces seem to come into play in similar manner, the increasing concentration of economic activity in a relatively small number of particular strong locations is less apparent. Instead of a clear core-periphery, a complex pattern emerges, in which the involved firms and their target choices are obviously driven rather by territorial neighbourship effects than by European-wide or global forces. Accordingly, even in the business of M&As – an agreed key mechanism of globalisation, often regarded as particularly footloose – geography matters and calls attention to one of the mysteries of the wireless (and wired) world in that, in some way, "physical presence counts even more than it used to" (The Economist 2002).

5 FINAL CONSOLIDATION AND CONCLUDING REMARKS

The analysis of corporate mergers and takeovers requires a multidirectional approach to understanding their determinations and impacts on a variety of issues such as the location of economic decision-making, the competitiveness, performance and evolution of firms and regions, or network and power relations on the different geographical scales. The contribution in hand has attempted to investigate in detail the implications of M&As on regional production systems in terms of the related shifts of corporate control and the factors that may explain the detected levels and patterns of firms extending their boundaries by means of M&As in Germany and Europe. This final section summarises the key findings of the three previous chapters and concludes by underlining the contributions of the study to the exisiting literature.

5.1 A place for space in M&As?

As revealed by the second chapter addressing the geography of M&As in Germany, corporate takeovers are fundamentally a large city phenomenon. The wave of M&As during the 1990s led to a major concentration of firms, company headquarters and economic activity in the most important urban areas, thus contributing to the economic take-off of the main metropoli of the German economy. Furthermore, the chapter has demonstrated that the bulk of M&A transactions involve companies already located in large urban centres or take place within the same region. Economic agglomeration and the concentration of political power came into view as key drivers behind the flows of M&As. Geographical distance emerged as a significant factor shaping the territorial distribution of M&As if considered in conjunction with agglomeration, suggesting that once agglomeration is controlled for, firms searching for an M&A target or partners to merge with tend to look in nearby rather than in distant locations. The number of further local socio-economic characteristics addressed in the analysis appears, in contrast, being encompassed by the inter-relationship between economic and social factors in large cities.

Taking, again, Germany as illustrative case and building on these explorations, the third chapter has explored the changes in the spatial distribution of M&As over time and across different industries. Particular attention was paid to industry-specific transformations and the varying location specifics between knowledge-intensive, so-called 'new economy' industries and more traditional, i.e. manufacturing sectors of the 'old' economy. In order to identify the logic behind changes in the location of economic activity and decision-making, the presence of economies of agglomeration and proximity, the degree of metropolitan interconnections or 'archipelago economies', an industry's tendency towards concentration in large urban metropolitan areas, and the just established role played by geographical distance were analysed across ten different industrial sectors. The results of this analysis indicate that the straightforward distinction between the old and the new economy is oversimplified and not sufficient to explain changes in the location of economic decision-making and activity across sectors. It was argued that corporate takeovers have to be conceived as relational processes that show distinct patterns and characteristics according to their local, institutional and above all industry-specific contexts. To account for the varying location specifics of different industries is therefore a task of particular importance for the exploration of corporate takeovers and their spatial logics in future research.

The results of the fourth chapter shifting attention to the European scale and addressed cross-border M&As in a more explicit manner have provided evidence that economies of proximity and agglomeration represent key drivers of M&As not only at the national level. Localised knowledge sources or capabilities are thus to be regarded significant determinants of cross-border corporate investments in the European M&A economy. Instead of distinct core-periphery characteristics, the European M&A economy reveals a more complex picture, in which the involved firms and their target choices are obviously driven rather by local neighbourship effects than by European-wide or global forces. Detecting the differentiated forces operating at the local level, geography has been shown to offer powerful explanations not only to the question where, but also on the reasons why firms merge or acquire other companies.

5.2 Contributions to the existing literature

Together, the analytical framework and the empirical work at the aggregate level constitute a point of departure for future research into the topic. Particular attention is then to be paid first and foremost to the knowledge-driven, large firms detected in the previous chapter. Provided that in-depth considerations of the interaction perspective of the approach suggested in the preceding chapter give further evidence that these corporations (referred to global players in the introduction) aim to combine both the reach of the global market through large-scale networking and the internalisation of capabilities created at the local level, they arguably are better re-defined as 'glocal players'.

All in all, the three pieces of research presented in this collection contribute to the existing literature in the following way:

> ➤ The examinations have addressed an important, but neglected area of interest on the economic geographical research agenda and provided a detailed empirical investigation of corporate merger and takeover activities in spatial perspective.

> ➤ M&A activities could be revealed to present a decisive mechanism for the increasing overall relevance and interconnection of cities and large metropolitan regions as control nodes of the world economy.

> ➤ The scope to which corporate mergers and acquisitions – an agreed key driver for the increasing transnationality of economic activities – are affected by localisation effects or economies of agglomeration and proximity turned out to be remarkable; thus, for the most part, M&As are still conducted rather 'down-to-earth'. In this manner, the results are relevant and challenging for the continuing globalisation debate.

> ➤ By arguing that firms extending their boundaries with the aid of a merger or an acquisition are driven not only by the attraction of market forces or the assets of the target company, but also by the endeavour to internalise knowledge competencies which result from localised capabilities created in regional economic systems, the work finally adds to the discourse on the firm and its conceptualisation in the discipline.

Through the combination of qualitative and quantitative empirical research at the macro- and the micro level, geography proved fruitful for illuminating the various forces at different scales when exploring the implications of M&As on economic systems on the one hand, and the factors behind the detected patterns on the other. Having in this way provided meaningful explanations why firms engage in M&As and thus contributed to a field of interest also central to managerial sciences or business economics, the insights of the present study might possibly provoke a minor shift in the 'balance of intellectual trade' (Maskell 2001) between economic geography and its neighbouring disciplines.

REFERENCES

Aliberti, V. and M.B. Green (2000) Canada's International Merger Activity for the Period 1971-1991: A Developmental, Geographic and Historical Perspective, *Geography Online* 1(2).

Anand, J. (1995) Horizontal Mergers in a Declining Industry: the Role of Firm Resources and Corporate Governance, in: Molz, E. (ed.) *Proceedings of the Annual Conference of the Administrative Sciences Association of Canada*, Policy Division. Windsor: 1-10.

Ashcroft, B. and J.H. Love (1993) *Takeovers, Mergers and the Regional Economy*. Edinburgh: Edinburgh University Press.

Audretsch, D.B. and M.P. Feldman (1996) R&D spillovers and the geography of innovation and production, *American Economic Review* 86: 630-640.

Augmon, T.B. and Lessard, D.R. (1977) Investor recognition of corporate international diversification, *Journal of Finance* 9: 1049-1055.

Avery, C., Chevalier, J. A. and S. Schaefer (1998) Why Do Managers Undertake Acquisitions? An Analysis of Internal and External Rewards for Acquisitiveness, *Journal of Law, Economics, and Organizations* 14(1): 24-43.

Bathelt, H. (1997) *Chemiestandort Deutschland. Technologischer Wandel, Arbeitsteilung und geographische Strukturen in der Chemischen Industrie*. Berlin: Edition Sigma-Bohn.

Bathelt, H. and J. Glückler (2002) *Wirtschaftsgeographie: Ökonomische Beziehungen in räumlicher Perspektive*. Stuttgart: UTB.

Bathelt, H. and J. Glückler (2003) Toward a relational economic geography, *Journal of Economic Geography* 3: 117-144.

Bathelt, H. and J.S. Boggs (2003) Toward a Reconceptualization of Regional Development Paths: Is Leipzig's Media Cluster a Continuation of or a Rupture with the Past?, *Economic Geography* 79(3): 265-293.

Bathelt, H. and K. Griebel (2001) Die Struktur und Reorganisation der Zulieferer- und Dienstleisterbeziehungen des Industriepark Höchst (IPH), *IWSG Working paper 02-2001*, Frankfurt/Main: Johann Wolfgang Goethe-Universität.

Beaverstock, J.V., Taylor P.J. and R.G. Smith (1999) A roster of world cities, *Cities* 16: 445-458.

Berkovitch, E. and M.P. Narayanan (1993) Motives for Takeovers: An Empirical Investigation, *Journal of Financial and Quantitative Analysis* 28(3): 347-362.

Berndt, C. (1998) Ruhr firms between dynamic change and structural persistence: globalization, the 'German model' and regional place-dependence, *Transactions of the Institute of British Geographers* 23(3): 331-352.

Bertrand, O., Mucchielli, J.-L. and H. Zitouina (2004) Location Choices of Multinational Firms: The Case of Mergers and Acquisitions, *HWWA Discussion paper 274*, Hamburg.

Böhmer, E. and Y. Löffler (1999) Kursrelevante Ereignisse bei Unternehmensübernahmen: Eine empirische Analyse des deutschen Kapitalmarktes, *Zeitschrift für betriebswirtschaftliche Forschung* 51(4): 299-324.

Bosman, M. and M. De Schmidt (1993) The geographical formation of international management centres in Europe, *Urban Studies* 30: 967-980.

Braudel, F. (1984) *The Perspective of the World*. London: Collins.

Brenton, P., Di Mauro, F. and M. Lücke (1999) Economic Integration and FDI: An Empirical Analysis of Foreign Direct Investment in the EU and in Central and Eastern Europe, *Empirica* 26: 95-121.

Bundeskartellamt (2001) *Bericht des Bundeskartellamtes über seine Tätigkeit in den Jahren 1999/00 sowie über die Lage und Entwicklung auf seinem Aufgabengebiet*. Bonn: Deutscher Bundestag.

Cairncross, F. (1997) *The death of Distance*. London: Orion.

Castells, M. (1989) *The Informational City*. London: Blackwell.

Castells, M. (1996) *The Information Age: Economy, Society and Culture. Vol. I: The Rise of the Network Society*. Oxford: Blackwell.

Castells, M. (1998) *End of millennium*. Oxford: Blackwell.

Chandler, A. (1977) *The visible hand*. Cambridge: Belknap.

Chapman, K. (2003) Cross-border mergers/acquisitions: A review and research agenda, *Journal of Economic Geography* 3(3): pp. 309-334.

Chapman, K. and H. Edmond (2000) Mergers/Acquisitions and Restructuring in the EU Chemical Industry: Patterns and Implications, *Regional Studies* 34(8): 753-767.

Clark, G.L. (1989) Remaking the maps of corporate capitalism: the arbitrage economy of the 1990s, *Environment and Planning A* 21: 997-1.000.

Clark, G.L. (1993) Costs and prices, corporate competitive strategies and regions, *Environment and Planning A* 25(1): 5-26.

Clark, G.L. and D. Wójcik (2003) An economic geography of global finance: ownership concentration and stock price volatility in German firms and Regions, *Annals of the Association of American Geographers* 93(4): 909-924.

Clegg, J. (1996) United States Foreign Direct Investment in the European Community: The Effects of Market Integration in Perspective, in: Burton, F., Yamin, M. and S. Young (Eds.) *The Changing European Environment*. London: Macmillan, 189-206.

Collis, D.J. (1991) A resource-based analysis of global competition: The case of the bearings industry, *Strategic Management Journal* 12: 49-68.

Cooke, T.E. (1988) *International Mergers and Acquisitions*. Oxford: Basil Blackwell.

Coyle, D. (1997) *The Weightless World. Strategies for Managing the Digital Economy*. London: Capstone.

Curry, B. and K. George (1983) Industrial concentration: A survey, *Journal of Industrial Economics* 31(3): 203-255.

Davies, S. and B. Lyons (1996) *Industrial Organisation in the European Union: Structure, Strategy and the Competitive Mechanism.* Oxford: Clarendon.

Dicken, P. and A. Malmberg (2001) Firm in Territories: A Relational Perspective, *Economic Geography* 77(4): 345-363.

Dicken, P. and S. Öberg (1996) The global context: Europe in a world of dynamic economic and population change, *European Urban and Regional Studies* 3: 101-120.

Dunning, J.H. (1977) Trade, Location of Economic Activity and the MNE: A Search for an Eclectic Approach, in Ohlin, B., Hesselborn, P.O. and P.M. Wijkman (eds.) *The International Allocation of Economic Activity* London: Macmillan, 395-418.

Dunning, J.H. (1979) Explaining changing patterns of international production: in defence of the eclectic theory, *Oxford Bulletin of Economics and Statistics* 41: 269-295.

Dunning, J.H. (1997) The European internal market programme and inbound foreign direct investment, *Journal of Common Market Studies* 35: 189-223.

Dunning, J.H. (1998) Location and the Multinational Enterprise: A Neglected Factor?, *Journal of International Business Studies* 29: 45-66.

Duranton, G. and D. Puga (2000) Diversity and specialisation in cities: Why, where and when does it matter?, *Urban Studies* 37(3): 533-555.

Duranton, G. and D. Puga (2001) From sectoral to functional urban specialisation, *Research Papers in Environmental and Spatial Analysis 68*, London: LSE.

Duranton, G. and D. Puga (2003) Micro-foundations of Urban Agglomeration Enconomies, *NBER Working paper 9931*, Cambridge.

Eberts, R. and D. McMillen (1999) Agglomeration Economies and Urban Public Infrastructure, in: Cheshire, P. and E.S. Mills (eds.) *Handbook of Regional and Urban Economics.* North Holland: Elsevier Science Publishers, 1455-1495.

Economic Intelligence Unit (1996) *International Mergers and Acquisitions.* New York: Economic Intelligence Unit.

Florida, R. (2002) *The Rise of the Creative Class and How It's Transforming Work, Leisure, Community and Everyday Life.* New York: Perseus.

Foss, K. (2001) Organizing Technological Interdependencies: A Coordination Perspective on the Firm, *Industrial and Corporate Change* 10: 151-178.

Foss, N.J. (1999) *Theories of the firm: Critical perspectives in economic organisation.* London: Routledge.

Fosseart, R. (2001) World Cities in a World System, *Hérodote* 105: 10-25.

Franks, J. and C. Mayer (2001) Ownership and Control of German corporations, *Review of Financial Studies* 14: 943-977.

Friedmann, J. (1986) The World City Hypothesis, *Development and Change* 4: 12-50.

Friedmann, J. (1995) Where we Stand: A Decade of World City Research, in: Knox, P.L. and P. J. Taylor (eds.) *World Cities in a World-System.* Cambridge: Cambridge University Press, 21-47.

Frost, S.T. (2001) The geographic sources of foreign subsidiaries' innovation. *Strategic Management Journal* 22(2): 101-123.

Fujita, M. and J.F. Thisse (1996) Economics of agglomeration, *Journal of the Japanese and International Economies* 10: 339-378.

Fujita, M., Krugman, P. and A.J. Venables (1999) *The Spatial Economy: Cities, Regions and International Trade.* Cambridge: MIT Press.

Gaughan, P.A. (2002) *Mergers, Acquisitions, and Corporate Restructurings.* New York: Wiley.

Gereffi, G. and M. Korzeniewicz (eds.) (1994) *Commodity Chains and Global Capitalism.* Westport: Praeger.

Gerke, W., Garz, H. and M. Oerke (1995) Die Bewertung von Unternehmensübernahmen auf dem deutschen Aktienmarkt, *Zeitschrift für betriebswirtschaftliche Forschung* 47(9): 805-820.

Gillespie, A., Richardson, R. and J. Cornford (2001) Regional development and the new economy. *European Investment Bank Papers,* 6(1): 109-131.

Glückler, J. (2001) Zur Bedeutung von Embeddedness in der Wirtschaftsgeographie, *Geographische Zeitschrift* 89: 211-26.

Gorton, G. and F. Schmid (1996) Universal banking and the performance of German firms, *NBER Working paper 5453,* Cambridge.

Grabher, G. (ed.) (1993) *The embedded firm. On the Socioeconomics of Industrial networks.* London: Routledge.

Grabher, G. (2001) Ecologies of Creativity: the Village, the Group, and the Heterarchic Organisation of the British Advertising Industry, *Environment & Planning A* 33: 351-374.

Grabher, G. (2002a) The Project Ecology of Advertising: Tasks, Talents, and Teams, in: Grabher, G. (ed.) Production in Projects. Economic Geographies of Temporary Collaboration, *Regional Studies* 36(3): 245-262.

Grabher, G. (2002b) Cool Projects, Boring Institutions: Temporary Collaboration in Social Context, in: Grabher, G. (ed.) Production in Projects. Economic Geographies of Temporary Collaboration, *Regional Studies* 36(3): 205-214.

Graef, P. (1998) Cyberspace and call centers. New patterns of location, outsourcing and reengineering of services in Germany, *Netcom* 12(4): 397-402.

Granovetter, M. (1985) Economic action and social structure: the problem of embeddedness, *American Journal of Sociology* 49: 323-334.

Green, M.B. (1990) *Mergers and acquisitions: geographical and spatial perspectives*. London and New York: Routledge.

Green, M.B. and S.P. Meyer (1997) International acquisitions: host and home country explanatory characteristics, *Geografiska Annaler* 79B(2): 97-111.

Grossman, G.M. and E. Helpman (1994) Endogenous innovation in the theory of growth, *Journal of Economic Perspectives* 8: 23-44.

Grossman, S.J. and O.D. Hart (1986) The Costs and Benefits of Ownership: A Theory of Vertical and Lateral Integration, *Journal of Political Economy* 94(4): 691-719.

Gugler, K., Mueller, D.C., Yurtoglu, B.B. and C. Zulehner (2003) The Effects of Mergers: An International Comparison, *International Journal of Industrial Organization* 21(5): 625-653.

Haas, H. D. and J. Scharrer (1999) Die deutsche Energiewirtschaft, in: Institut für Länderkunde (ed.) *Nationalatlas Bundesrepublik Deutschland: Band 1. Gesellschaft und Staat*. Heidelberg: Spektrum, 118-121.

Haas, H.-D. and H.-M. Zademach (2005): Wertschöpfung und Handel im Textil- und Bekleidungsgewerbe vor dem Hintergrund der Internationalisierung und der Wirkung der Welttextilabkommen, *Geographische Rundschau*, 2005(2), forthcoming.

Hall, P. (1993) Forces shaping urban Europe, *Urban Studies* 30: 883-898.

Hassink, R. 2003. "Quiet" Restructuring in the Ordinary Region. A Case Study of the Textile Industry Cluster in Westmünsterland, Germany, Paper presented at the *RGS-IBG International Annual Conference*, London.

Healy, P.M., Palepu, K.G. and R.S. Ruback (1992) Does Corporate Performance Improve after Mergers?, *Journal of Financial Economics* 31(2): 135-175.

Henderson, J., Dicken, P., Hess, M., Coe, N., and H.W-C. Yeung (2002) Global production networks and the analysis of economic development, *Review of International Political Economy* 9(3): 436-464.

Hess, M. (2004) „Spatial" Relationships? Re-conceptualising embeddedness, *Progress in Human Geography* 28(2): 165-186.

Hudson, R. and E.W. Schamp (1995) *Towards a New Map of Automobile Manufacturing in Europe? New Production Concepts and Spatial Restructuring*. Berlin: Springer.

Hymer, S. (1960) *The International Operations of National Firms: A Study of Direct Investment*. Cambridge: MIT.

Jaffe, A.B., Trajtenberg, M. and Henderson, R. (1993) Geographic localization of knowledge spillovers as evidenced by patent citations, *Quarterly Journal of Economics* 108: 577-598.

Jansen, S.A. (2000) *Mergers & Acquisitions: Unternehmensakquisition und -kooperation*. Wiesbaden: Gabler.

Jansen, S.A. (2001) Pre- und Post Merger-Integration bei grenzüberschreitenden Zusammenschlüssen, in: Jansen, S.A., Picot, G. and D. Schiereck (eds.) *Internationales Fusionsmanagement. Erfolgsfaktoren grenzüberschreitender Zusammenschlüsse.* Stuttgart: Schäffer-Poeschel, 3-33.

Jansen, S.A. (2002) Schlechtwetterfront oder globaler Klimawechsel? Ein Jahr danach: Der M&A-Markt nach dem 11. September 2001, *M&A Review* 2002(10), editorial.

Jansen, S.A., Picot, G. and D. Schiereck (eds.) (2001) *Internationales Fusionsmanagement. Erfolgsfaktoren grenzüberschreitender Zusammenschlüsse.* Stuttgart: Schäffer-Poeschel.

Jensen, M.C. and R.S. Ruback (1983) The Market for Corporate Control. The Scientific Evidence, *Journal of Financial Economics* 11: 5-50.

Kang, N.-H. and S. Johansson (2000) Cross-Border Mergers and Acquisitions: Their Role in Industrial Globalisation, *OECD STI Working paper 2000/1*, Paris: OECD.

Kelly, K. (1998) *New rules for the New Economy.* London: Fourth Estate.

Krätke, S. (2001) Berlin – Towards a Global City?, *Urban Studies* 38(10): 1777-1800.

Krätke, S. (2002) Network Analysis of Production Clusters: The Potsdam/Babelsberg Film Industry as an Example, *European Planning Studies* 10(1): 27-54.

Krätke, S. (2003) Global Media Cities in a Worldwide Urban Network, *European Planning Studies* 11(6): 605-628.

Krugman, P. (1991) *Geography and Trade.* Cambridge: MIT.

Krugman, P. (1995) *Development, Geography, and Economic Theory.* Cambridge: MIT.

Kuemmerle, W. (1999) Foreign direct investment in industrial research in the pharmaceutical and electronics industries. Results from a survey of multinational firms, *Research Policy* 28: pp. 179-193.

Lagendijk, A. (1995) The foreign takeover of the Spanish automobile industry: a growth analysis of internationalisation, *Regional Studies* 29: 381-393.

Leamer, E. and M. Storper (2001) The Economic Geography of the Internet Age, *Journal of International Business Studies* 32(4): 641-665.

Lo, V. (1999) Der M&A-Markt in Deutschland, *Working paper SFB 403 AB-99-24*, Frankfurt/Main: Johann Wolfgang Goethe-Universität.

Lo, V. (2000) Netzwerke im Mergers&Acquisitions-Geschäft, *Working paper SFB 403 AB-00-18*, Frankfurt/Main: Johann Wolfgang Goethe Universität.

Lo, V. (2003) *Wissensbasierte Netzwerke im Finanzsektor. Das Beispiel des Mergers& Acquisitions-Geschäfts.*Wiesbaden: Gabler.

Lorenzen, M. and V. Mahnke (2002) Global strategy and the acquisition of local knowledge – How MNCs enter regional knowledge clusters, Paper presented at the *DRUID Summer Conference on Industrial Dynamics of the New and Old Economy,* Copenhagen 2002.

Loughran, T. and A.M. Vij (1997) Do Long-Term Shareholders benefit from Corporate Aquisitions?, *Journal of Finance* 52: 1765-1790.

Markusen, A.L. (1994) Studying Regions by studying firms, *The Professional Geographer* 46(4): 477-490.

Markusen, A.L. (2001) An Actor-Centered Approach to Economic Geography, Paper presented at the *Conference of Global Economic Change*, Worcester: Clark University.

Martin, R., Miller, P. and S. Mayes (2003) The New Economy: Myths, Realities and Regional Dynamics, Paper presented at the *Workshop on High-Tech Business: Clusters, Contraints and Economic Development*, Cambridge: Robinson College.

Martin, R. (2000) Institutional Approaches in Economic Geography, in: Sheppard, E. and T.J. Barnes (eds.) *A Companion to Economic Geography*. Oxford: Blackwell, 77-94.

Martin, R. (2002) From the Old Economy to the New Economy. Myths, Realities and Geographies, Paper presented at the *Regional Studies Association Conference on Geographies of the New Economy*, London: RGS.

Martin, R. and P. Sunley (1996) Paul Krugman's Geographical Economics and Its Implications for Regional Development Theory: A critical Assessment, *Economic Geography* 72(3): 259-292.

Martin, R. and P. Sunley (2003) Deconstructing Clusters: Chaotic Concept or Policy Panacea?, *Journal of Economic Geography* 3(1): 5-35.

Maskell, P. (2001) The Firm in Economic Geography, *Economic Geography* 77(4): 329-344.

Maskell, P. and A. Malmberg (1999) Localised Learning and Industrial Competitiveness, *Cambridge Journal of Economics* 23: 167-185.

Maskell, P., Bathelt, H. & Malmberg, A. (2004) Temporary Clusters and Knowledge Creation: The Effects of International Trade Fairs, Conventions and Other Professional Gatherings. *Spaces 2004-04*, Marburg: Philipps-University, Faculty of Geography.

Maskell, P., Eskelinen, H., Hannibalsson, I., Malmberg, A. and E. Vatne (1998) *Competitiveness, localised learning and regional development: Specialisation and prosperity in small open economies*. London: Routledge.

Mergers & Acquisitions (M&A) (2001) Mergers & Acquisitions in Fakten und Zahlen (http://www.m-and-a.de, accessed January 2001).

Mergers & Acquisitions (M&A) (2003) M&A-Fakten: Entwicklung der Unternehmen nach Branchen (http://www.m-and-a.de, accessed September 2003).

Monopolkommission (2003) *Netzwettbewerb durch Regulierung. Hauptgutachten 2000/01*. Baden Baden: Nomos.

Morgan, K. (2004): The exaggerated death of geography: learning, proximity and territorial systems, *Journal of Economic Geography* 4: 3-21.

Morosini, P. (2001) Managing cross-cultural M&As: Today's organizational imperative is how to win in execution, in: Jansen, S.A., Picot, G. and D. Schiereck (eds.) *Internationales Fusionsmanagement. Erfolgsfaktoren grenzüberschreitender Zusammenschlüsse.* Stuttgart: Schäffer-Poeschel, 131-150.

Narin, F., Hamilton, K.S. and D. Olivastro (1997) The increasing linkage between U.S. technology and public science, *Research Policy* 26: 317-330.

Nilsson, J.E. and E.W. Schamp (1996) Restructuring of the European production system: processes and consequences, *European Urban and Regional Studies* 3: 121-132.

Niman, N.B. (2004) The evolutionary firm and Cournot's Dilemma, *Cambridge Journal of Economics* 28: 273-289.

Nuhn, H. (1999a) Fusionsfieber – Neuorganisation der Produktion in Zeiten der Globalisierung, *Geographie und Schule* 21: 16-22.

Nuhn, H. (1999b) Konzentrationsprozesse in der Milchwirtschaft Norddeutschlands – Wirtschaftsräumliche Grundlagen und Auswirkungen, *Berichte zur deutschen Landeskunde* 73(2/3): 165-190.

Nuhn, H. (2001) Megafusionen - Neuorganisation großer Unternehmen im Rahmen der Globalisierung, *Geographische Rundschau* 53 (7/8): 16-24.

Nuhn, H. (2004) Konzentrationsprozesse in der Wirtschaft, in: Institut für Länderkunde (ed.) *Nationalatlas Bundesrepublik Deutschland: Band 9. Unternehmen und Märkte*, Heidelberg: Spektrum, 54-55.

ÒhUhallachàin, B. (1994) Foreign Banking in the American Urban System of Financial Organization, *Economic Geography* 70(3): 206-228.

O'Brien, R. (1992) *Global financial integration: the end of geography.* London: Royal Institute of Financial Affairs.

Organisation for Economic Co-operation and Development (OECD) (1996) *Globalisation of Industry: Overview and Sector Reports.* Paris. OECD.

Organisation for Economic Co-operation and Development (OECD) (2000) *OECD Economic Outlook, June 2000.* Paris: OECD.

Penrose, E.T. (1959) *The Theory of the growth of firms.* New York: Oxford University Press.

Picot, G. (2000) *Handbuch Mergers and Acquisitions - Planung, Durchführung, Organisation.* Stuttgart: Schäffer-Pöschel-Verlag.

Porter, M.E. (1990) *The Competitive Advantage of Nations.* New York: Free Press.

Porter, M.E. (1998) Clusters and the new economics of competition, *Harvard Business Review* 76(6): 77-90.

Pratt, A. (2000) New media, the new economy and new spaces, *Geoforum* 31: 425-436.

Quah, D.T. (1996) The invisible hand and the weightless economy, *Occasional paper No. 12*, London: Centre for Economic Performance.

Quah, D.T. (1997) Increasingly weightless economies, *Bank of England Quarterly Bulletin* 2: 49-56.

Ravenscraft, D. and F. Scherer (1987) *Mergers, Sell-offs and Economic Efficiency*. Washington DC: Brookings Institution.

Rigby, D.L. (2000) Geography and Technological Change, in: Sheppard, E. and T.J. Barnes (eds.) *A Companion to Economic Geography*. London: Blackwell, 202-223.

Robinson, G.M. (1998) *Methods and Techniques in Human Geography*. Chichester: John Wiley.

Rodríguez-Pose, A. (1998) *Dynamics of Regional Growth in Europe: Social and Political Factors*. Oxford: Oxford University Press.

Rodríguez-Pose, A. (1999) Innovation prone and innovation averse societies: Economic performance in Europe, *Growth and Change* 30: 75-105.

Rodríguez-Pose, A. (2002) *The European Union: Economy, Society, and Policy*. Oxford: Oxford University Press.

Sachwald, F. (ed.) (1994) *European Integration and Competitiveness*. Aldershot: Edward Elgar.

Sassen, S. (1984) The New Labor Demand in Global Cities, in: Smith, M.P. (ed.) *Cities in Transformation*. Beverly Hills: Sage, 139-171.

Sassen, S. (1990) *The mobility of labor and capital. A study in international investment and labor flow*. Cambridge: Cambridge University Press.

Sassen, S. (1991) *The Global City: New York, London, Tokyo*. Princeton: Princeton University Press.

Sassen, S. (2000) *Cities in a World Economy*. London: Pine Forge Press.

Saxenian, A.L. (1994) *Regional Advantage*. Cambridge: Harvard University Press.

SBA (US Small Business Administration) (1998) *Mergers and acquisitions in the United States, 1990-1994 - an analysis of business acquisition activity by firm size and industry* (http://www.sba.gov/advo/stats/m_a.html, accessed January 2001).

Schamp, E. (2000) *Vernetzte Produktion. Industriegeographie aus institutioneller Perspektive*. Darmstadt: Wissenschaftliche Buchgesellschaft.

Schamp, E.W. (2003) Raum, Interaktion und Institution – Anmerkungen zu drei Grundperspektiven der deutschen Wirtschaftsgeographie, *Zeitschrift für Wirtschaftsgeographie* 47(3/4), pp.145-158.

Scott, A.J. (1988) *New industrial spaces: Flexible production Organization and Regional Development in North America and Western Europe*. London: Pior.

Scott, A.J. (1996) The craft, fashion, and cultural product industries of Los Angeles: competitive dynamics and policy dilemmas in a multisectoral image-producing complex, *Annals of the American Association of Geographers* 86: 306-323.

Sekkat, K. and O. Galgau (2001) The Impact of the Single Market on Foreign Direct Investment in the European Union, Paper presented at the *International Conference on Exchange Rate Regimes, Economic Integration, and the International Economy*, Toronto: Ryerson University.

Shan, W. and J. Sang (1997) Foreign direct investment and the sourcing of technology advantages: An evidence from the biotechnology industry, *Journal of International Business Studies* 28: 267-284.

Shinn, E.W. (1999) Returns to acquiring firms: The role of managerial ownership, managerial wealth, and outside owners, *Journal of Economics and Finance* 23(1): 78-89.

Shleifer, A. and R.W. Vishny (1989) Management Entrenchment: The Case of Manager-Specific Investments, *Journal of Financial Economics* 25: 123-139.

Srinivasan, K. and A. Mody (1997) Location Determinants of Foreign Direct Investment: An empirical Analysis of US and Japanese Investment, *Canadian Journal of Economics* 30(2): 778-799.

Storper, M. (1997) *The Regional World. Territorial Development in a Global Economy.* New York: Guilford Press.

Storper, M. and A.J. Venables (2004) Buzz: The Economic Force of the City, *Journal of Economic Geography* 4: 351-370.

Storper, M. and R. Walker (1989) *The Capitalist Imperative. Territory, Technology, and Industrial Growth.* New York: Basil Blackwell.

Streeck, W. (1997). German capitalism: Does it exist? Can it survive, in: Crouch, C. and W. Streeck (eds.) *Political Economy of Modern Capitalism: Mapping Convergence and Diversity.* London: Page, 33-54.

Sunley, P. (2000) Urban and Regional Growth, in: Sheppard, E. and Barnes, T.J. (eds.) *A Companion to Economic Geography.* London: Blackwell, 187-201.

Taylor, M.J. and B. Asheim (2001) The Concept of the Firm in Economic Geography, *Economic Geography* 77(4): 315-328.

Taylor, M.J. (2004) The Firm as a Connected, Temporary Coalition. *Spaces 2004-05*, Marburg: Philipps-University, Faculty of Geography.

Taylor, P.J. (2000) World Cities and Territorial States under Conditions of Contemporary Globalization, *Political Geography* 19(1): 5-32.

Taylor, P.J. (2001) Specification of the world city network, *Geographical Analysis* 33: 181-194.

Taylor, P.J. (2003) Recasting World-Systems Analysis: City Networks for Nation-States, in Dunaway, W.A. (ed.) *Emerging Issues in the 21st Century World-System Vol II New Theoretical Directions for the 21st Century World-System.* Westport, CN: Praeger, 130-40.

Taylor, P.J., Catalano, G. and N. Gane (2002a) A Geography of Global Change: Services and Cities, 2000-01, *GaWC Research Bulletin 77*, Loughborough.

Taylor, P.J., Catalano, G. and D.R.F. Walker (2002b) Measurement of the world city network, *Urban Studies* 39(13), 2367-2376.

The Economist (2002) Press the flash not the keyboard. In a wired world, physical presence counts more than ever, *The economist print edition*, August 22nd 2002 (www.economist.com/business/Printerfriendly.cfm?Story_ID=1291480, accessed September 2004).

Thomson Financial (2003) *Mergers & Acqusitions Report* (http://www.mareport.com, accessed August 2003).

Trautwein, F. (1990) Merger Motives and Merger Prescription, *Strategic Management Journal* 11: 283-295.

United Nations (UN) (1995) *World Investment Report 1994: Transnational Corporations, Employment and the Workplace.* New York and Geneva: UN.

United Nations (UN) (2000) *World Investment Report 2000. Cross-border Mergers and Acquisitions and Development.* New York and Geneva: UN.

United Nations (UN) (2002) *World Investment Report 2002. Transnational Corporations and Export Competitiveness.* New York and Geneva: UN.

United Nations (UN) (2003) *World Investment Report 2003. FDI Policies for Development: National and International Perspectives.* New York and Geneva: UN.

United Nations (UN) 2000. *World Investment Report 2000. Cross-border Mergers and Acquisitions and Development.* New York: UN.

United Nations Conference on Trade and Development (UNCTAD) (2000) Survival in global business arena as key driver of cross-border mergers and acquisitions boom, *Press release TAD/INF/2855* (http://r0.unctad.org/en/press/pr2855en.htm, accessed September 2003)

Uppenberg, K. and A. Riess (2004) Determinants and growth effects of foreign direct investment, *EIB papers* 9(1): 52-84.

Veltz, P. (1996) *Mondialisation, Villes et Territoires: l'économie d'archipel.* Paris: Presses Universitaires de France.

Veltz, P. (2000) European cities in the world economy, in: Bagnasco, A. and P. Le Galès (eds.) *Cities in contemporary Europe.* Cambridge: Cambridge University Press, 33-47.

Veltz, P. (2004) The rationale for a resurgence in the major cities of advanced economies, Paper presented at the *Leverhulme International Symposium*, London: LSE.

Venables, A.J. (1998) The assessment: Trade and location, *Oxford Review of Economic Policy* 14: 1-6.

Werneck, T. (1998) *Deutsche Direktinvestitionen in den USA. Determinanten und Wirkungen am Beispiel der Bundesstaaten Georgia, North Carolina und South Carolina* (= Wirtschaft & Raum, Band 1), München: VVF.

Weston, J.F., Siu, J.A. and B.A. Johnson (2001) *Takeovers, Restructuring and Corporate Governance*. New Jersey: Prentice Hall.

Williamson, O.E. (1975) *Markets and hierarchies: analysis and antitrust implications*. New York: Free Press.

Williamson, O.E. (1985) *The Economic Institutions of Capitalism. Firms, Markets, Relational Contracting*. New York: Free Press.

Wójcik, D. (2002) The Länder are the building blocks of the German capital market, *Regional Studies* 36: 877-895.

Wójcik, D. (2003) Change in the German model of corporate governance: evidence from blockholdings 1997-2001, *Environment & Planning A* 35: 1431-1458.

Wrigley, N. (1999) Corporate finance, leveraged restructuring and the economic landscape: the LBO wave in US food retailing, in: Martin, R. (ed.) *Money and the Space Economy*. Chichester: Wiley, 185-205.

Yeung, H.W. (2000) Organizing 'the firm' in industrial geography I: Networks, institutions and regional development, *Progress in Human Geography* 24(2): 301-315.

Yeung, H.W. (2001a) Does Economics Matter for/in Economic Geography? *Antipode* 33(2): 168-175.

Yeung, H.W. (2001b) Regulating 'the firm' and sociocultural practices in industrial geography II, *Progress in Human Geography* 25(2): 293-302.

Yeung, H.W. (2002) Producing 'the firm' in industrial geography III: Industrial restructuring and labour markets, *Progress in Human Geography* 26(3): 366-378.

Young, S., Hood, N. and E. Petters (1994) Multinational enterprises and regional economic development, *Regional Studies* 28: 657-677.

Zademach, H.-M. (2001) Regionalökonomische Aspekte der M&A-Transaktionen mit deutscher Beteiligung (1990-1999) – Ergebnisse einer Zeitreihen- und Regressionsanalyse, *M&A Review* 2001(12): 554-563.

Zademach, H.-M. (2002) 'The Firm in Economic Geography' – zu einer integrierten Konzeption der Unternehmung. *Munich Business Research 2002-08*, Munich: LMU.

Zademach, H.-M. (2004) Unternehmenszusammenschlüsse und -übernahmen, in: Institut für Länderkunde (ed.) *Nationalatlas Bundesrepublik Deutschland*. Heidelberg: Spektrum, 56-57.

Zeller, C. (2000) Rescaling power relations between trade unions and corporate management in a globalising pharmaceutical industry: the case of the acquisition of Boehringer Mannheim by Hoffman-La Roche, *Environment & Planning A* 32(9): 1545-1567.

APPENDIX

Appendix 1: M&A specifics across industry sectors: Regression results 118

Appendix 2: Interviewed firms and institutions (in alphabetic order) 121

Appendix 3: Interview Guideline 122

Appendix 4: Preparation of Mergermarket database 126

Appendix 5: M&A transactions in Europe, 1998-2003 127

Appendix 6: European M&A activities (1998-2003), as estimated via location
quotient *MApC-I* 128

Appendix 7: Results of bivariate correlations on the European scale 129

Appendix 1: M&A specifics across industry sectors: Regression results

Dependent variable: M&A	ln GDP_i	ln GDP_j	ln $Dist_{ij}$	R^2
a.) Financial Services (n = 1905)				
1990	0.296	0.195	- 0.098	0.130
1991	0.221	0.133	- 0.082	0.070
1992	0.028 n.s.	0.126	- 0.010 n.s.	0.016
1993	0.275	0.146	- 0.065	0.098
1994	0.297	0.144	- 0.076	0.111
1995	0.296	0.190	- 0.106	0.128
1996	0.271	0.215	- 0.075	0.119
1997	0.304	0.203	- 0.084	0.134
1998	0.292	0.251	- 0.100	0.150
1999	0.275	0.208	- 0.067	0.118
b.) Insurance (n = 316)				
1990	0.120	0.125	- 0.045	0.030
1991	0.103	0.101	- 0.061	0.023
1992	0.184	0.141	- 0.058	0.055
1993	0.141	0.143	- 0.019 n.s.	0.040
1994	0.139	0.146	- 0.048	0.041
1995	0.110	0.113	- 0.029 n.s.	0.025
1996	0.151	0.158	- 0.042	0.047
1997	0.188	0.106	0.006 n.s.	0.046
1998	0.152	0.118	- 0.021 n.s.	0.036
1999	0.152	0.104	- 0.041 n.s.	0.034
c.) Transport (n = 566)				
1990	0.182	0.128	- 0.062 n.s.	0.051
1991	0.211	0.134	- 0.048	0.063
1992	0.151	0.081	0.036 n.s.	0.031
1993	0.142	0.082	- 0.050	0.028
1994	0.192	0.142	- 0.026 n.s.	0.056
1995	0.142	0.162	- 0.035 n.s.	0.046
1996	0.192	0.132	- 0.021 n.s.	0.053
1997	0.163	0.093	- 0.061	0.037
1998	0.137	0.114	- 0.046	0.032
1999	0.150	0.105	- 0.019 n.s.	0.033
d.) Media (n = 744)				
1990	0.177	0.096	- 0.008 n.s.	0.040
1991	0.143	0.022 n.s.	- 0.001 n.s.	0.021
1992	0.164	0.118	- 0.018 n.s.	0.040
1993	0.162	0.124	- 0.087	0.047
1994	0.122	0.160	- 0.048	0.041
1995	0.150	0.174	- 0.040 n.s.	0.052
1996	0.133	0.168	0.012 n.s.	0.045
1997	0.165	0.174	- 0.009 n.s.	0.056
1998	0.170	0.177	- 0.031 n.s.	0.059
1999	0.170	0.164	- 0.011 n.s.	0.054

Observations: 1560 (without transactions within the same region)
Degrees of Freedom: 3, 1556

Notes: n.s.: not significant (10%-level); all coefficients are standardized

Appendix 1: M&A specifics across industry sectors: Regression results (cont.)

Dependent variable: M&A	ln GDP_i	ln GDP_j	ln $Dist_{ij}$	R^2
e.) ICT (n = 457)				
1990	0.160	0.092	- 0.034 n.s.	0.034
1991	0.176	0.145	- 0.017 n.s.	0.051
1992	0.147	0.096	- 0.015 n.s.	0.030
1993	0.096	0.069	0.000 n.s.	0.014
1994	0.170	0.138	- 0.089	0.053
1995	0.187	0.176	- 0.073	0.068
1996	0.184	0.161	- 0.023 n.s.	0.058
1997	0.208	0.182	- 0.068	0.077
1998	0.183	0.168	- 0.024 n.s.	0.058
1999	0.180	0.198	- 0.028 n.s.	0.070
f.) Heavy Manufacturing (n = 542)				
1990	0.179	0.123	- 0.042	0.047
1991	0.222	0.024 n.s.	- 0.049	0.051
1992	0.186	0.068	- 0.063	0.042
1993	0.134	0.050	- 0.052	0.022
1994	0.193	0.112	- 0.064	0.052
1995	0.194	0.077	- 0.088	0.049
1996	0.144	0.100	- 0.149	0.049
1997	0.128	0.087	- 0.058	0.026
1998	0.136	0.121	- 0.097	0.040
1999	0.087	0.095	- 0.042	0.017
g.) Automotive (n = 348)				
1990	0.127	0.055	- 0.034 n.s.	0.020
1991	0.162	0.029 n.s.	- 0.043	0.028
1992	0.183	0.037 n.s.	- 0.016 n.s.	0.035
1993	0.130	0.076	- 0.072	0.027
1994	0.133	0.106	- 0.089	0.035
1995	0.132	0.099	- 0.045	0.028
1996	0.132	0.104	- 0.081	0.033
1997	0.111	0.107	- 0.008 n.s.	0.023
1998	0.112	0.061	- 0.017 n.s.	0.016
1999	0.125	0.047	- 0.020 n.s.	0.018
h.) Energy (n = 1026)				
1990	0.161	0.122	- 0.111	0.051
1991	0.176	- 0.007 n.s.	- 0.074	0.036
1992	0.170	- 0.024 n.s.	- 0.032 n.s.	0.031
1993	0.151	0.074	- 0.189	0.061
1994	0.210	0.089	- 0.177	0.079
1995	0.166	0.044	- 0.199	0.065
1996	0.150	0.136	- 0.162	0.062
1997	0.170	0.103	- 0.205	0.076
1998	0.179	0.107	- 0.169	0.067
1999	0.133	0.071	- 0.138	0.039

Observations: 1560 (without transactions within the same region)
Degrees of Freedom: 3, 1556

Notes: n.s.: not significant (10%-level); all coefficients are standardized

Appendix 1: M&A specifics across industry sectors: Regression results (cont.)

Dependent variable: M&A	$\ln GDP_i$	$\ln GDP_j$	$\ln Dist_{ij}$	R^2
i.) Chemicals (n = 1051)				
1990	0.260	0.118	-0.065	0.083
1991	0.185	0.063 n.s.	-0.036 n.s.	0.038
1992	0.229	0.079	-0.013 n.s.	0.058
1993	0.219	0.125	-0.024 n.s.	0.062
1994	0.210	0.123	-0.072	0.062
1995	0.255	0.150	-0.060 n.s.	0.087
1996	0.188	0.126	-0.082	0.054
1997	0.199	0.177	-0.094	0.075
1998	0.227	0.165	-0.047	0.078
1999	0.126	0.092	-0.038 n.s.	0.025
j.) Textiles (n = 148)				
1990	0.098	0.053	-0.010 n.s.	0.012
1991	0.055	0.022 n.s.	-0.025 n.s.	0.004
1992	0.098	0.014 n.s.	-0.012 n.s.	0.010
1993	0.032 n.s.	0.024 n.s.	-0.035 n.s.	0.003 n.s.
1994	0.094	0.076	-0.083	0.020
1995	0.057	0.045	-0.008 n.s.	0.005
1996	0.054	0.064	-0.039 n.s.	0.008
1997	0.038 n.s.	0.087	-0.038 n.s.	0.010
1998	0.064	0.066	-0.082	0.014
1999	0.075	0.086	-0.007 n.s.	0.013

Observations: 1560 (without transactions within the same region)
Degrees of Freedom: 3, 1556

Notes: n.s.: not significant (10%-level); all coefficients are standardized

Appendix 2: Interviewed firms and institutions (in alphabetic order)

Name of firm or institution	Position of interview partner	Location
Dr. Fried & Partner (Managment Consultancy)	Managing Director	Munich (D)
Fiege Deutschland (Logistics)	Head of Purchasing	Headquarter, Münster/Greven (D)
French Government Agency for Internat. Investment	Director	French Ambassy, London (UK)
Handelsblatt Group of Publishers (Media)	Head, Invetment Management	Headquarter, Dusseldorf (D)
Invest in Bavaria	Managing Director	Munich (D)
Mergermarket	M&A Analyst	Headquarter, London (UK)
Mergermarket	CEO	Headquarter, London (UK)
Royal Danish Ministry of Foreign Affairs	Project Manager	Copenhagen
Valtech (ICT)	Business Development	Headquarter, Dusseldorf (D)

Appendix 3: Interview guideline

SPATIAL DYNAMICS IN THE MARKETS OF M&AS –
On the geographical determination and implications of corporate takeovers and mergers in Germany and Europe

A research project of the Munich School of Management,
Institute of Economic Geography, Ludwig-Maximilians-University,
Ludwigstr. 28, D-80539 Munich

Supported by the German Research Foundation DFG (HA 795/8-1)

May 2004 to August 2005

Principal investigator:	Prof. Dr. Hans-Dieter Haas
Research Fellow:	Hans-Martin Zademach, MSc
Contact:	Phone: +49 (0)89 2180 2688
	Fax: +49 (0)89 2180 3809
	Email: Zademach@bwl.uni-muenchen.de

Information about this interview

Name of Firm:	Interviewer:
Date:	Location:
Remarks:	

1. Introductory questions

- Please sketch a picture of your company (size, turnover, age etc.) and enumerate the approximate share of your company's revenue generated abroad.
- Do you follow a specific internationalisation strategy? Or does your company's focus predominantly lie on the home market.

In how many mergers or acquisitions have you been engaged? Which one was the most important [recent] one? Were these local, national, continental or intercontinental?

Please give a brief general description of the most important / recent transaction you have been involved in (particularly in terms of its motivation, challenges and implications).

[If the interview partner has been involved in more than one transaction:
- ➤ To what extent do you observe similarities / differences between each individual transaction?
- ➤ What is your opinion: Does each M&A transaction present a single and individual case, or are – at least to a certain extent – also some characteristics of standardisation applicable / observable?]

2. On the relevance of markets / locations and the spatial determination of M&A transactions

Where and on which scale are the investments of your company / group undertaken?

At which locations and in which areas (regions, but also business segments) disinvestments are made?

How do you evaluate the relevance of a buyer's following individual objectives in terms of their relevance for an M&A transaction?

- ➤ Please a) specify the most important factors by weight and
    b) evaluate them by marks.

	Five most important: (1 [most important], 5 [least important])	Evaluation by mark: (10 [very important] to 1 [unimportant])
a.) General / competition related objectives		
- increasing the company's valuation		
- growth		
- reducing competitive threats		
- reducing the risk of becoming a take-over target		
b.) Production oriented goals		
- economies of scale		
- economies of scope		

123

(continued)

- decreasing dependence on suppliers/ customers
- access to new technologies

c.) Market related objectives
- completion of product ranges
- increase of market share
- access to new markets / customer groups
- acquisition of brand name / image

d.) Increasing management's power

e.) Tax optimisation

f.) Increasing the target's market valuation

Are there any further objectives not considered here? What about the presence of firms in the same sector, clients and competitors?

How do you evaluate the role of culture and language, legal frameworks, previous knowledge of the target market or previous contacts with the executives of the target company?

How are markets / locations of potential targets analysed and potential targets assessed?

Does, in your opinion, geographical distance (proximity) play a role in M&A activities? [If yes: what distance do you still consider as 'close'? Which are the concrete advantages of spatial / geographical proximity?]

3. Interrelation between location-specific factors and the company's growth / development

What has been, to your assessment, the actual impact of the target's location / region economic power on the decision in favour of the specific target?

How do economies of agglomeration (i.e. a common labour pool, endowments of infrastructure, human capital, transport systems etc.) express themselves for the involved companies?

The following questions are related to some results of previous investigations:

In the hitherto conducted studies on M&As on the aggregated level, agglomeration economies, geographical distance and political power of a target's location proved as significant variables with regard to the territorial distribution of M&As. To what extent do you agree?

Socio-economic factors (such as the educational level of a target region's population, its share of employees in the service sector, investment in R&D, unemployment rates, urbanity in general etc.), on the other side, turned out as less significant. What is your estimation in this regard?

To what extent do you consider the industry sector as an important influencing factor on the various specifics of M&As?

4. The impact of M&As on regional economic systems

Which are, to your appraisal, the effects of M&As on regional structures, economic systems or the spatial organisation of production?

How did the M&A transaction you have been involved in interact on the interrelations and dependencies on the local level? To what extent do institutional re-arrangements or organisational restructuring provoke implications in this regard?

Did 'your' M&A transaction resulted in major changes concerning the network relations (e.g. associations with suppliers or customers) of the involved firms / actors in the corresponding localities?

To what extent has your global location and production network been affected by suchlike transactions?

In the remaining final questions we are interested in your opinions and estimations as person concretely involved in / affected by M&A transactions, i.e. with according experiences:

How do, in your notion, M&A transactions impact on regional disparities?

Does the intensified transnational (metropolitan) interconnectivity via cross-border deals relate to the process of European integration; in which direction (in terms of causality)?

5. Concluding remarks

Any further comments?

Thank you very much for your time and efforts.

Appendix 4: Preparation of Mergermarket database

Original database		
Completed transactions, 1998-2003		**18,633**
Preparation for analysis		
Number of 'split' transactions	1,189	
(as either more than one target country or/and more than one bidder country are involved)		
Number of added transactions due to splitting		1,763
		20,396
Events without European involvement	4,944	
Final number of events obtained		**15,452**

Appendix 5: M&A transactions in Europe, 1998-2003

(by country)	as bidder		as target		balance (bidder - target)		bidder / target	
	events (in %)	Σ vol.[1] (in %)	events (in %)	Σ vol.[1] (in %)	by events	by volume[1]	by events	by vol.
Austria	204 (1.54)	13,579.9 (0.31)	149 (1.16)	20,809.3 (0.55)	55	-7,229.4	1.37	0.65
Belgium	299 (2.25)	65,225.0 (1.51)	284 (2.22)	61,216.4 (1.63)	15	4,008.5	1.05	1.07
Cyprus	5 (0.04)	591.7 (0.01)	6 (0.05)	218.0 (0.01)	-1	373.7	0.83	2.71
Czech Rep.	32 (0.24)	3,264.8 (0.08)	115 (0.90)	14,967.3 (0.40)	-83	-11,702.5	0.28	0.22
Denmark	244 (1.84)	34,018.3 (0.79)	253 (1.98)	37,533.8 (1.00)	-9	-3,515.5	0.96	0.91
Estonia	4 (0.03)	114.5 (0.00)	19 (0.15)	378.8 (0.01)	-15	-264.3	0.21	0.30
Finland	289 (2.18)	59,046.1 (1.36)	246 (1.92)	49,624.2 (1.32)	43	9,421.9	1.17	1.19
France	1,306 (9.83)	648,060.8 (14.96)	1,169 (9.13)	476,611.7 (12.7)	137	171,449.1	1.12	1.36
Germany	1,352 (10.2)	590,188.1 (13.63)	1,543 (12.1)	632,209.7 (16.8)	-191	-42,021.6	0.88	0.93
Greece	87 (0.65)	12,208.7 (0.28)	68 (0.53)	10,776.5 (0.29)	19	1,432.2	1.28	1.13
Hungary	38 (0.29)	3,671.4 (0.08)	75 (0.59)	8,823.3 (0.23)	-37	-5,151.8	0.51	0.42
Iceland	22 (0.17)	1,257.9 (0.03)	9 (0.07)	505.7 (0.01)	13	752.2	2.44	2.49
Ireland	250 (1.88)	24,829.1 (0.57)	217 (1.70)	32,556.5 (0.87)	33	-7,727.3	1.15	0.76
Italy	929 (6.99)	391,818.7 (9.05)	915 (7.15)	405,811.3 (10.8)	14	-13,992.6	1.02	0.97
Latvia	2 (0.02)	36.4 (0.00)	14 (0.11)	1,700.9 (0.05)	-12	-1,664.4	0.14	0.02
Liechtenstein	3 (0.02)	328.5 (0.01)	4 (0.03)	2,048.5 (0.05)	-1	-1,719.9	0.75	0.16
Lithuania	4 (0.03)	117.4 (0.00)	24 (0.19)	1,529.4 (0.04)	-20	-1,412.0	0.17	0.08
Luxembourg	80 (0.60)	23,282.3 (0.54)	44 (0.34)	24,274.8 (0.65)	36	-992.5	1.82	0.96
Malta	4 (0.03)	299.8 (0.01)	5 (0.04)	319.3 (0.01)	-1	-19.5	0.80	0.94
Netherlands	908 (6.83)	248,901.3 (5.75)	696 (5.44)	195,129.6 (5.19)	212	53,771.7	1.30	1.28
Norway	238 (1.79)	47,024.5 (1.09)	323 (2.52)	56,312.0 (1.50)	-85	-9287.5	0.74	0.84
Poland	65 (0.49)	6,752.0 (0.16)	195 (1.52)	23,985.7 (0.64)	-130	-17,233.7	0.33	0.28
Portugal	92 (0.69)	17,820.1 (0.41)	126 (0.98)	18,268.7 (0.49)	-34	-448.6	0.73	0.98
Slovakia	10 (0.08)	188.0 (0.00)	47 (0.37)	9,141.6 (0.24)	-37	-8,953.6	0.21	0.02
Slovenia	5 (0.04)	107.2 (0.00)	16 (0.13)	2,185.8 (0.06)	-11	-2,078.6	0.31	0.05
Spain	599 (4.51)	248,603.2 (5.74)	687 (5.37)	191,301.1 (5.09)	-88	57,302.2	0.87	1.30
Sweden	602 (4.53)	113,331.9 (2.62)	511 (3.99)	112,504.7 (2.99)	91	827.2	1.18	1.01
Switzerland	455 (3.42)	134,102.9 (3.10)	329 (2.57)	93,760.8 (2.49)	126	40,342.1	1.38	1.43
UK	5158 (38.8)	1,642,604 (37.9)	4,710 (36.8)	1,274,775 (33.9)	448	367,828.8	1.10	1.29
Total	**13,286 (100)**	**4,331,374 (100)**	**12,799 (100)**	**3,759,280 (100)**	**487**	**572,094**	**1.04**	**1.15**

Note: [1] in million Euro

Appendix 6: European M&A activities (1998-2003), as estimated via location quotient $MApC\text{-}I$

	$MApC\text{-}I_{(gdp)}$			
	as bidder		as target	
	(by number of events)	(by volume)	(by number of events)	(by volume)
Austria	0.697	0.142	0.528	0.251
Belgium	0.856	0.573	0.844	0.620
Cyprus	0.363	0.132	0.452	0.056
Czech Republic	0.348	0.109	1.298	0.575
Denmark	1.003	0.429	1.079	0.545
Estonia	0.445	0.039	2.195	0.149
Finland	1.572	0.985	1.389	0.954
France	0.645	0.982	0.599	0.832
Germany	0.471	0.631	0.558	0.778
Greece	0.479	0.206	0.388	0.210
Hungary	0.480	0.142	0.983	0.394
Iceland	1.840	0.323	0.781	0.149
Ireland	1.649	0.503	1.486	0.759
Italy	0.556	0.719	0.568	0.858
Latvia	0.171	0.010	1.241	0.513
Liechtenstein	0.790	0.265	1.094	1.907
Lithuania	0.222	0.020	1.380	0.299
Luxembourg	2.732	2.438	1.559	2.929
Malta	0.714	0.164	0.926	0.201
Netherlands	1.576	1.325	1.254	1.197
Norway	0.965	0.585	1.360	0.807
Poland	0.257	0.082	0.799	0.335
Portugal	0.555	0.330	0.789	0.390
Slovakia	0.307	0.018	1.500	0.993
Slovenia	0.165	0.011	0.549	0.255
Spain	0.673	0.857	0.802	0.760
Sweden	1.728	0.998	1.523	1.141
Switzerland	1.204	1.089	0.904	0.877
United Kingdom	2.430	2.374	2.303	2.123

Appendix 7: Results of bivariate correlations on the European scale

	M&A (counts) [Poisson]	ln M&A (Σ volumes) [OLS]
ln *GDP*	0.702**	0.383**
ln *POP*	0.746**	0.266**
ΔGDP	-0.051**	-0.282**
ln *GDP/cap*	0.524**	0.312**
ln *Patents*	0.493**	0.389**
ln *Pat/cap.*	0.524**	0.305**
Education	0.002*	-0.085
Unemployment	0.029**	-0.045
ln *Distance*	-0.882**	-0.257**
Neighbour	1.450**	0.266**
Investment climate	-0.344**	-0.191**
Language	1.207**	0.190**
EU15	1.646**	0.312**
EFTA	-0.729**	-0.019
New members	1.789**	-0.325**
EMU	0.753**	0.223**

Note: ** and * denote significance at the 0.01 and 0.05 level respectively

Wirtschaft und Raum

Eine Reihe der Münchener Universitätsschriften

herausgegeben von

Prof. Dr. Hans-Dieter Haas
Universität München

Band 13: Michael Oechsle: **Erweiterung von Geschäftsfeldern im Non-Aviation-Bereich an europäischen Flughäfen unter besonderer Berücksichtigung des Standorts München**
2005 · 400 Seiten · ISBN 3-8316-0544-0

Band 12: Hans-Martin Zademach: **Spatial Dynamics in the Markets of M&A** · Essays on the Geographical Determination and Implications of Corporate Takeovers and Mergers in Germany and Europe
2005 · 150 Seiten · ISBN 3-8316-0478-9

Band 11: Johannes Rehner: **Netzwerke und Kultur** · Unternehmerisches Handeln deutscher Manager in Mexiko
2004 · 268 Seiten · ISBN 3-8316-0352-9

Band 10: Norbert Schultes: **Deutsche Außenwirtschaftsförderung** · Ökonomische Analyse unter Berücksichtigung der Aktivitäten und Programme in Japan
2003 · 304 Seiten · ISBN 3-89481-452-7
wieder lieferbar ab ca. 01/2006

Band 9: Petra Oexler: **Citylogistik-Dienste** · Präferenzanalysen bei Citylogistik-Akteuren und Bewertung eines Pilotbetriebs dargestellt am Beispiel der dienstleistungsorientierten Citylogistik Regensburg (RegLog(r))
2002 · 418 Seiten · ISBN 3-89481-450-0
vergriffen – kein Nachdruck geplant

Band 8: Eckhard Störmer: **Ökologieorientierte Unternehmensnetzwerke** · Regionale umweltinformationsorientierte Unternehmensnetzwerke als Ansatz für eine ökologisch nachhaltige Wirtschaftsentwicklung
2001 · 410 Seiten · ISBN 3-8316-8410-3

Band 7: Jochen Scharrer: **Internationalisierung und Länderselektion** · Eine empirische Analyse mittelständischer Unternehmen in Bayern
2001 · 231 Seiten · ISBN 3-8316-8407-3

Band 6: Romed Kelp: **Strategische Entscheidungen der europäischen LKW-Hersteller im internationalen Wettbewerb**
2000 · 231 Seiten · ISBN 3-8316-8390-5

Band 5: Mathias von Tucher: **Die Rolle der Auslandsmontage in den internationalen Wertschöpfungsnetzwerken der Automobilhersteller**
1999 · 270 Seiten · ISBN 3-8316-8369-7

Band 4: Claudia Lübbert: **Qualitätsorientiertes Umweltschutzmanagement im Tourismus**
1999 · 275 Seiten · ISBN 3-89481-359-8
vergriffen – kein Nachdruck geplant

Band 3: Christian Michael Schwald: **Religionsgeprägte Weltkulturen in ökonomischen Theorien**
1999 · 228 Seiten · ISBN 3-8316-8355-7

Band 2: Martin Heß: **Glokalisierung, industrieller Wandel und Standortstruktur – das Beispiel der EU-Schienenfahrzeugindustrie**
1998 · 218 Seiten · ISBN 3-8316-8335-2

Band 1: Till Werneck: **Deutsche Direktinvestitionen in den USA – Determinanten und Wirkungen am Beispiel der Bundesstaaten Georgia, North Carolina und South Carolina**
1998 · 298 Seiten · ISBN 3-8316-8334-4

Erhältlich im Buchhandel oder direkt beim Verlag:
Herbert Utz Verlag GmbH, München
089-277791-00 · info@utzverlag.de

Gesamtverzeichnis mit mehr als 2500 lieferbaren Titeln: www.utzverlag.de